The Spirit of "The Book;" or, Memoirs of Caroline Princess of Hasburgh,

THE SPIRIT OF "THE BOOK;" OR, MEMOIRS OF CAROLINE *PRINCESS OF HASBURGH,*

A Political and Amatory Romance.

IN THREE VOLUMES.

VOL. II.

EDITED BY

THOMAS ASHE, Esq.

"The Book"---Any Person having in their Possession a CERTAIN BOOK, printed by Mr. Edwards in 1807, but *never published*, with W. Lindsell's Name as the Seller of the same on the Title Page, and will bring it to W. Lindsell, Bookseller, Wimpole-Street, will receive a handsome Gratuity.——TIMES Paper, 27 *March* 1809.

LONDON:

PRINTED AND PUBLISHED BY ALLEN & CO.
NO. 15, PATERNOSTER-ROW.

1811.

LETTER XXVIII.

CAROLINE *to* CHARLOTTE.

AT breakfast I was treated by my father with peculiar tenderness and affection: nor did Algernon escape his notice; he conversed with him with unusual affability: enquïred into the success of his embassy to Berlin, and desired to know whether, during his stay at Paris he had visited the French Pantheon. I understand,' continued my father, 'that it is dedicated—" To "great men, by their faithful country." —'Pray, sir, can you give us any account of it? Your friends here will 'be interested in the recital, and Caroline who, appears so poorly this morning, may be amused and instructed by 'your report.'

"Yes, my Prince," returned Algernon with his accustomed grace and timidity, "this dedicatory inscription is "in the highest degree impressive, and "speaks in forcible accents to the soul "of every man of sensibility. But "alas! the pleasing impression we feel "on reading it is weakened and almost "obliterated by the galling remem-"brance that we have seen the con-"secration of that temple profaned by "the corps of the infamous Marat re-"posing near the honored remains of "Rousseau. That act has made the "edifice a monument of the incorrigi-

" ble fickelness and folly of the French, " It is a disgrace to the nation.—From " the day that the corps of Marat en- " tered the Pantheon, it seems as if its " fatal influence had marked the build- " ing out for ruin, such as the monster " himself once threatened to bring " down on universal France.—QUATER- " MERE, however, who has the chief " direction of this building, seems to " augur differently; and in a report " which he has presented to the Direc- " tory he answers to the charge of in- " congruity in the alterations, and de- " clares that the Pantheon, noble, at " least, as a poetical conception, is, in " fact, less the abode of death than of " immortality. It is not so much a hy- " pogeum, whose grave and serious " forms should announce the silence " of the grave, as a temple open for the " worship of great men. In short, al- " though no individual be admitted to

" the honors of the place till after his " death, he receives them rather under " the form of apotheosis and philoso- " phic consecration than under the " emblems of mortality.

" Besides, the catacombs of the Pan- " theon, on becoming the repository " of the ashes of Voltaire and Rous- " seau, have been consecrated as a " place of repose for the inanimate re- " mains of great men.—The afflictive " idea that those peaceful cells have " been sullied by the corps of Marat, " fills the soul with disgust and horror. " I still saw there the broken sarcopha- " gus that enclosed his vile carcase, " but which, loaded with the male- " dictions of the people was transport- " ed to a church-yard where his de- " tested remains were consumed with " lime. The bones of Mirabeau yield- " ed their station to Marat, and have " been placed in a spot, on which a

" mark has been set. In another corner
" of the same recess, appears an empty
" sarcophagus, which has been destined
" for General Dampierre; but the de-
" cree which granted him the honors of
" the Pantheon, has been revoked.

" The two sarcophagi which contain
" the mortal remains of Rousseau and
" Voltaire, are placed opposite to each
" other in the middle of the vault.
" They are of wood and covered with
" basso-relievos, but are hereafter to be
" succeeded by others in black marble.
" On the tomb of Rousseau is engraved
" the simple and beautiful epitaph,
" taken from the tomb in the Isle of
" Poplars by Ermenonville; 'HERE
" RESTS THE MAN OF NATURE AND OF
" TRUTH.'—On each of the two narrow
" sides of the sarcophagus, appears a
" hand of Death holding a torch, and
" as it were issuing from the tomb.—
" This was intended as a symbol—

"though poorly enough devised—to "express the idea that the philosopher "has shed light on the world after his "death: a poet might have employed "it with success, but it was not at all "fit for the statuary: the pair of hands "starting from the tomb excite a "disagreeable sensation.—The sarco-"phagus of Voltaire is loaded on every "side with prolix inscriptions, which "recount his actions and his deserts in "a great profusion of words, and in a "style by no means suited to monu-"mental records. When the whole "work is completed, sepulchral lamps "are to be kept burning night and "day in these vaults, and will impart "an air of greater majesty to these "mansions of the dead.

"The ashes of Descartes are also "preserved in this repository of na-"tional monuments; they are inclosed

" in a small sarcophagus of porphyry
" exquisitely wrought in the Egyp-
" tian manner, which the Count de
" Caylus brought from Italy, and
" which bears this simple inscription—
" ' ASHES OF DESCARTES.'

" But,"—observed the dear Algernon, who himself appeared faint and exhausted,—" I fear I go too much " into detail: it may fatigue you to " attend to me so long, and perhaps " the Princess Caroline would prefer " the open air perhaps—" ' No, no,' reiterated my father,—' proceed Alger- ' non, your narration affords the great- ' est pleasure. Proceed, I command ' you proceed.'

Algernon turned his eyes on me, and perceiving a pensive smile of approbation, thus pursued his elegant narrative.

"The attic of this gigantic edifice is "supported by twenty-two fluted co- "lumns of the Corinthian order, above "the portico, and was filled with a "mystical basso relievo, representing "the Triumph of Faith. This has "been removed: and the COUNTRY, "distributing civic crowns to Virtue "and Genius is the subject of the new "decorations which are in unison with "the import of the beautiful inscrip- "tion on the portico.—Basso relievos "are over the great gate of the temple: "the declaration of the Rights of "Man: Nature holding the Table of "the Law exposed to view; near her, "Liberty and Equality. Public in- "struction—Minerva arrayed in a long "robe of Peace, with her right hand "extended, presents a crown to a "youth, who clings to the goddess.— "Above this group: to a crowd of pa- "rents, accompanied by their children,

"THE COUNTRY presents the INSTITU-
"TRESS distributing public instruction,
"with this inscription—'Instruction
"is necessary to all; society owes it
"alike to all her members.'—Group on
"the opposite side of the parvis:—
"Dying for one's country: a female fi-
"gure representing THE COUNTRY,
"supports a naked and wounded war-
"rior, who, dying leans on his buck-
"ler, covered with a lion's skin. Her
"looks, attentively fixed on him, are
"expressive of maternal tenderness.—
"The genius of Glory sustains a sol-
"dier who falls expiring at the altar
"of the country, on which he deposits
"his sword.—On the right stands
"an image of the Law. This figure,
"in a sitting posture, with an air of
"command, and with the greatest se-
"riousness in her expression and atti-
"tude, has her right hand extended,
"grasping a general's truncheon, while

" her left is placed on the Tables of
" the Law, on which are engraved
" these words;—' Mankind are equal
" by Nature, and in the eye of the
" Law! Another group; THE COUN-
" TRY presents the law to the people,
" as the expression of the general will.
" An aged senior bends the knee be-
" fore the law; a soldier swears to de-
" fend her Inscription: 'Under the
" government of the LAW, innocence is
" secure.'

" But no description can equal the
" grandeur and attractive beauty of the
" perspective of the façade, the parvis,
" and the dome, which majestically
" crowns them. Indeed it is impos-
" sible to pass by this edifice without
" stopping to enjoy the noble coup
" d'œil which it presents, and feeling
" the pleasing sensations awakened by
" the inscription—' To GREAT MEN,

" THEIR GRATEFUL COUNTRY.' And " by the figure of a Hercules in a rest- " ing attitude, with this inscription— " 'Strength through the Law.'—And " another: THE COUNTRY, seated at " the gate of the Temple of the Law, " points out to Innocence, the statue " of Justice; and to Oppression the " statue of Humanity!—The execu- " tion of this group," continued Algernon looking alternately upon my father and upon me, " is adequate to the " dignity of the idea; the expression " is eloquent; the effect is grand. It " secures justice to the innocent, and " humanity to the oppressed. It—"

My father rose—looked at his watch, resumed his seat, and desired Algernon to proceed. But he was weary; and perceived, that his manner of expressing the inscriptions of 'Mankind are equal by Nature'—' Under the government of the Law Innocence is secure,' &c. &c. had occasioned me so much anguish of mind, that I was on the point of discovering myself by my emotion; but recollecting how much was at stake I endeavoured to conceal my feelings; and soon after Algernon had ceased, I left the room to abandon myself to a sorrow which at this distant period renders me incapable to pursue my present train of reflections.

Farewell then!

CAROLINE.

LETTER XXIX.

SEVERAL days elapsed, my dear Charlotte, without any event occurring calculated to rouse the feelings, or to interest the mind. It was evident, however, that the grand catastrophe was not only anticipated, but beginning, and that nothing could arise capable to obstruct the proposed union with the Marquis of Albion; a man whom I never beheld.

During this tedious interval, I seldom saw Algernon. Every thing, therefore, was tame and languid: and the plot against my happiness was creeping on without any attempt to overcome, or disturb the rapidity of its progress.

As if destitute of passion to engage sympathy, or of interest to excite exertion, things were thus advancing to a gigantic maturity, when, one evening after supper, Algernon addressed my father with a faltering voice, and a look clouded with pensiveness. "Sir," said he, "I am miserable enough to "want a favor of you, but I have "hardly strength of mind to ask it. "Having long experienced your boun-"ty and munificence, I might make "an enomium on your goodness and "humanity, but I shall not, Sir, pay "so bad a compliment to your under-"standing, as to endeavour by flattery, "to win it over to my interest; the "favor is, Sir, that during this degrad-"ing peace with France, you will al-"low me to retire from your service

" and to visit my own country; and " that, whenever you take the field, " you will recal me to partake of your " glory, or to perish nobly by your " side.

" Here, Sir," continued Algernon with an emotion which passed like an electric shock thro' every heart, " here " Sir, is the sword which you present- " to me on the day that I severed the " head of a Hussar, while he aimed " a blow at your life. Take your " sword, Sir, it is somewhat damaged, " it is true; it is hacked and lustreless; " it has been bathed in the blood of " your enemies, in the service of my " Prince; it has been used, General, " but never sullied! Do not," said he, after a short pause, which no person had courage to interrupt, " do not ima- " gine that I resign it through fear. " Without having the blood of Princes

" in my veins, I feel, flowing in them, " the crimson stream of honor. Algernon knows not fear! But why " do I assert this. I appeal to you, " my General, and ask, did you ever " see Algernon turn his horse's head " to save his life? Did Algernon ever " aspire to a higher ambition than to " fight in the cause of your country, " or to perish in the field of battle?"

Here the mind of the Duke was restored to all its amiable and original qualities; he rose with a countenance at once illuminated with delight, and clouded by sorrow, and clasping Algernon in his arms, blessed and applauded him as a youth of unparalleled intrepidity and honor.

Under the impression of this interesting scene, and the melancholy tidings of Algernon's departnre for his native country, I sunk into the bosom of Melina, and was conducted by her, and by Prince L——s, into a freer air.

Algernon did not come to my assistance. Released from the affectionate arms of my father, he cast himself into a chair, and hid the emotion of his feelings by holding his handkerchief to his eyes. On my return, I found him neither altered in situation nor in condition. My father, however, soon roused him from so pensive and painful a state of sensibility, by observing to him, 'that 'it was a matter of surprize how he 'could think of returning to a country 'which many of the English people re- 'present as the most worthless and fe- 'rocious of any existing. And yet,' continued my father, 'I cannot reconcile 'this account with my own particular 'experience; many officers of your 'nation serve with me, and they have

'always afforded the most praisewor-
'thy example as fellow-citizens; of
'laudable and decided ambition as sol-
'diers, and of considerable and diver-
'sified merit as men. Do, Sir, recon-
'cile such contradictions if you possi-
'bly can, and above all let me know,
'how a people who are said to be hos-
'pitable, liberal, and addicted to po-
'etry and music, can be so savage and
'brutal as the English ministerial wri-
'ters exhibit them to the world?'

"Alas! Sir," replied the amiable Algernon, awaking out of the pensive state into which he was cast after the delivery of his sword; "alas! Sir, it is the
"interest of the vile portion of those
"writers to revile my countrymen, be-
"cause they wish to enervate, if not
"to extinguish the Irish constitution,
"to cramp their legislative independ-
"ence, and to confine the liberties of

" the people! In order, then, to convert
" Ireland into a headless and a heart-
" less trunk: in order to take away
" the body and soul of the Irish peo-
" ple; to annihilate their rights; to
" wither their capacities, and their
" prospects; these illiberal and insi-
" dious writers think it necessary to
" represent them as a people of savage
" manners, depraved hearts and blot-
" ted intellects, and incapable of the
" government of their own affairs.
" This accounts to your Highness for
" all that odium which is said to stain
" our national character. But, Sir, it
" is needless to advance further argu-
" ments on this point; I prefer to sub-
" mit a few observations in evidence,
" that hospitality, and a love of poetry
" and letters, are qualities which the
" Irish people are generally allowed.

" It is undoubtedly true, Sir, as you " have observed, that in the pastoral " song and ballad, the Irish greatly " excel. In artless expressions of pas- " sion, truth of colouring, and naiveté " of diction, nothing can rival their " pastoral songs. They originated in " a country abounding in a rich assem- " bly of rural images; smooth and lofty " hills, covered with verdure; clear " streams winding through long and " beautiful vallies; trees produced " without culture, here straggling or " single, and there crowding into little " groves and bowers; with other cir- " cumstances peculiar to the country, " which rendered them fit for pastur- " age, and eminently favorable to ro- " mantic leisure and tender passions. " Several of the old Irish songs take " their names from the rivulets, rivers, " and hills adjoining to the Shannon " near the Lake of Killarney; a region

" distinguished by many charming va-
" rieties of rural scenery, and which,
" whether we consider the face of the
" country, or the genius of the people,
" may properly be termed the arcadia
" of Ireland. And all these songs are
" sweetly and powerfully expressive of
" love and tenderness, and other emo-
" tions suited to the tranquillity of
" rural life.

" To rouse the imagination by the
" charms of novelty, the life of the
" Irish peasantry is full of events which
" strike the fancy, and when clothed
" in the metaphorical and exuberant
" language of poetry, cannot fail to in-
" terest our curiosity, and excite our
" feelings. In short, Sir, the inde-
" pendence, hospitality, and love of
" poetry among the Irish, are beautiful
" features of their character, and form
" a strong contrast with the more lux-

" urious and servile existence of the
" people by whom they are abused."

'But admitting,' interrupted my father, 'that your countrymen have all 'this simplicity of sentiment and manner, and the hospitality which render them a people so superior and 'interesting, what can you, my young 'friend, do amongst them? You! who 'are accustomed to the agitation of a 'camp and the enjoyments of a court, 'what can you do in a country which 'can present you nothing but scenes 'of still life, and objects of rude and 'vulgar simplicity?'

"Whatever may be thought, Sir," exclaimed Algernon, with enthusiasm, "of rural life, it is, nevertheless, my "opinion, that a taste for the pure and "simple pleasures of the country, procures a superior enjoyment to all the

" glory and happiness to be found " either in camps or in courts. When " I return to the land of my fathers, " I shall pass my time in labour, plea- " sure, and rest, each in moderate " quantity, in equal parts, and suc- " cessively exchanged. My life shall " be an uninterrupted chain of pensive " moments, for labour itself, a labour " suited to my circumstances and " strength, and unaccompanied with " ambitious ingredients, will be ac- " companied with a kind of calm plea- " sure, the beneficial influence of " which must diffuse itself throughout " my whole being. But to enjoy this " natural happiness, it is necessary, Sir, " to preserve the greatest of the gifts " of nature, and those by which we " receive all others—it is necessary to " preserve our natural feelings uncor- " rupt; and thus to preserve them, it "is indispensibly requisite to think "humanely, humbly, and justly!"

Algernon paused. 'Continue,' said my father, with some emotion, 'continue! though not quite well, I take 'pleasure in your designs. Continue!'

After casting a timid glance around, Algernon thus continued——

"I shall, Sir, take up my abode in "my father's house, which is seated "in a pleasant valley formed by nature to afford an asylum to a small "number of rural persons, who know "but little of the unnatural and corrupt manners of a more exposed "world. There I will live content, "and, though limited to the little circle "of the common comforts of life, endeavour to make myself and others

" happy. While yet a boy, I there " planted a honey-suckle bower. It " must now be in full growth. When " showers fall upon the teeming earth, " and give a sweeter smell to the love- " ly flowers that adorn the valley, I " will there enjoy a book. At other " times, I will take my rod, and fish " on those silver streams, that glide " silently towards their centre, the tem- " pestuous sea; and again I will visit " that tempestuous sea to call to my " remembrance the storms and the " tempests which now distract me!"

'You sketch with a liberal and glow- ' ing pencil, Algernon,' said my father, ' but my young friend, your imagina- ' tion is too enthusiastic and warm! ' What storms and tempests are you ' exposed to? Have you not experien- ' ced the friendship of my family and ' the protection of my state? Your re-

'proaches cannot be interpreted into 'ingratitude—tell me, then, what are 'the sources of your complaints?'

"O, Sir!" exclaimed Algernon, "you "have named the cause of my regret, "it is but too true, that I possess a "warm and an enthusiastic mind!"

'That I believe,' said the Duke, 'but you have mentioned your father, 'it is now too late; I am, however, 'curious to hear you describe his cha-'racter and mode of life; to-morrow, 'after breakfast, you must indulge us 'with an account of his life.'

We thus soon separated, and will you believe it, my Charlotte, I separated from my Algernon with none but sentiments of joy and exultation in my heart! And why?—Good God! and why, with sentiments of joy and exulıtion? My child! I shall tell you. Vhile attending to Algernon's account f his country; to the place he intend- d to retire to, and to the life he in- ɜnded to lead, I came to a resolu- on to fly with him; to abandon my 'iends and my country, and to partici- ate in his truly innocent and happy esigns!! To give him my hand, and ɔ place it beyond the disposal of any ther power upon earth!

The instant I formed this determina- on, my spirits assumed their usual ɜrenity; pleasure flowed into my heart, ıd excited a train of delightful associ- .ions, which dispelled the gloom and ıelancholy which so long pervaded and ırkened my expression. I only long- ꞁ to hear the memoirs of the father f my Algernon, and then for an op- ɔrtunity of unfolding to him the design I had formed in his favor. For the realization of such hopes, I refer you, my sweet girl, to my next letter.

CAROLINE.

LETTER XXX.

With unaffected ease, natural expression, great brilliancy of fancy, and some persuasion from all the breakfast party, Algernon, at the appointed time, gave the following description of his father, whom he distinguished by the simple appellation of a moral character.

"Sequestered from the tumults of
" towns, a gentleman of my father's
" philosophic temper and ideas, finds
" abundantly in all seasons of the year,
" to recreate his imagination in the
" country. There does he delight him-
" self with amiable reveries, which,
" though unconnected, as wandering
" about the varieties of the creation,

" are, notwithstanding, lighted up by " the beauties of moral truth. One " time, following the current of a rivu- " let, which serpentinely glides in the " plain, and which, notwithstanding " the windings, it appears to assume " for securing and prolonging its exist- " ence, is soon swept away by its natu- " ral declivity into some neighbouring " river; he thinks, that so it is, the " days of human life flow on, and that " in spite of all our endeavours to slack- " en their too rapid course, every in- " stant of time robs us of a part of our- " selves, and leads us into the bound- " less ocean of eternity.

" Another time, observing at a dis- " tance the ardours of the chace, amidst " the sound of echoing horns, and the " eager pursuit of hounds, he cannot " help detesting those violent and un- " just men, those enemies of the re-

" pose of mankind, who, intoxicated " by their excesses, will know no " other law than that of brutality and " force!

" The humble cottage covered with " turf, and coated with sedge, reminds " him that so many cares cannot inha- " bit there as in gilded palaces!

" That flock, which skips and bounds " on the green carpet of the earth, re- " vives in him the happy times of in- " fancy, when man was unacquainted " with all the other passions, but the " transports of innocence and integrity.

" In the tender cares of that yew for " her lambkins, he acknowledges the uni- " versality of that law of nature, which " was the first bond of society among " men. He still plainly sees in it the " infinite wisdom of a first being atten-

" tive to watch over the preservation of " the host of his creatures. At this " sight, his soul, divided between ad- " miration and gratitude, is intirely ab- " sorbed by the sentiments they inspire " him with.

" From the top of the hill, whence " he descries the different landscapes " terminated by the horizon, he loves " to descend into the valley by a rugged " and steep inclination. And his con- " templation is succeeded by a cursory " view of new and enchanting objects. " 'O nature!' cries he, 'what variety " do I discover in thy work! Thou " knowest neither line, nor level, nor " compass; but the irregularity and " negligence thou appearest to affect far, " far indeed, exceed the contemptible " symmetry of the works of man!'

"He treads under foot tufts of violets, "and the cool breezes waft all around "him fragrant odours. What pencil "has discriminated the variegated co- "lours of the flowers of his meadow? "The primroses, cowslips, and daisies, "by which it is enamelled, were not "purchased by weight of gold in fo- "reign climates to be distributed in the "contours of gay parterres. He prizes "them as the gifts of bounteous na- "ture, and they are more delightful in "his eyes than the produce of bulbous "roots of the most curious Dutch "florist.

"What gradations are observable in "the verdure, with which the earth "arrays the vegetables that shoot out "of its bosom! He thinks and medi- "tates on that subject, and then calls "out to those, who pretend that no- "thing in nature is hidden to them, to "tell him the salts that discriminate "the green tint of the poplar, from that "of the humble herb or blade of grass? "'Point out to me,' he says, 'all the "intermediate differences. But what "am I about to ask? I consult man, "and I forget that man is only made "to enjoy and to admire?'

"Does not my father's spring, that "source of pure water, at the foot of "the mountain, afford him a draught "of the truest salubrity? It has not, "indeed, that taste so pleasing to the "palate as the fermented juices of "fruits, yet has it not their pernicious "effects; and when he quenches his "thirst with it, his reason neither loses "its light, nor its serenity. When he "climbs the mountain before his fru- "gal repast, a new scene ravishes and "enchants him. What serenity in "the air! What brightness in the sun!

" Or if some darksome spots are ob-
" served around, they are shadows that
" heighten the beauties of picturesque
" nature. Such must have been the
" day, when the being that created the
" world, was pleased to take a view of
" his work after its passing out of dark-
" ness and chaos. On that day, the
" purple morn came smiling to open
" with her rosy fingers the gates of the
" east. On that day, the sun by his
" piercing rays vivifying the world, gave
" colours and soul to all different be-
" ings.

" So every thing assumed a smiling
" aspect all over the plain as far as my
" father's prospect extends, and the
" emulous echoes repeat the songs they
" heard in faithful modulations. After
" such days the star that adorns the
" night, has often to warn the good
" old man to return to his hamlet, and

" he returns with a heart as pure as " the days he spends in his fields.

" What are his thoughts at the " sight of his blooming orchards! The " perfume they exhale, borne on the " wings of Zephyrs, embalm the at- " mosphere.—'Ah!' says he, 'can ' this greatest beauty of nature retain ' but a momentary existence? Ye ten- ' der flowrets, how few of you will es- ' cape the fury of the northern blast? ' But do not complain, ye are not the ' only subjects to rigorous destiny. I ' have seen a young plant rise in the ' centre of a flower-bed; I have seen ' it shoot up in strength; it was one ' day to be the glory and ornament of ' my garden; I took pleasure in culti- ' vating it; the rays of sound reason ' already illustrated the morning of its ' days; yes, its calix was ready to ' blossom and to bloom; but I sud-

'denly saw it transplanted : it is now 'an exotic in another clime ; perhaps 'it is faded—or, perhaps it is dead !'

"Alas ! 'tis me ! 'tis Algernon he "means ! Cease, father ! cease your "tears—your son is on his return, and "will again strive to make your garden "a scene of unmingled delight !

"The sun, ready to go down, seems "to participate his course and shines "with new splendour !—Scarce has he "stooped under the horizon, when "night spreads her sable mantle "throughout the spaces of our hemis- "phere.

'Ye mortals,' then exclaims my father, 'closing this scene of contempla- 'tion, do not dread to be buried in 'darkness: athwart that ancient forest, 'and at the surface of our globe, I see 'another luminary breaking forth, to 'share with the night the empire of 'the sky.—In cities its light will only 'second wicked deeds: In the coun'try it is the life and soul of innocent 'pleasures, to which the sound of the 'pipe has given an invitation after the 'long labours of the day.—So it is, 'that nature presents us with true 'pleasures, the source of which is as 'pure as the author of our desires; 'but art, in compact with our vices, 'by its factitious pleasures seduces the 'desire; and, false sages as we are, 'by endeavouring to be more than 'men, we lose the sense of huma'nity.'

"Then the respectable old man "rises, and gives the signal for re"treat."

‘ Go, happy friends,’ he says, ‘go ‘ and enjoy the sweets of repose ’till ‘ the lark wakes you with the dawn of ‘ day. Dread not being disturbed by ‘ troublesome dreams; ’tis criminal, ‘ turbulent, ambitious life only that ‘ generates them; for you, sleep ‘ has provided the sweetest pop- ‘ pies; go, and providence be with you!’

“ Such is my father, Sir,” continued Algernon.

And such is ‘ *the man of nature and* ‘ *of truth,*’ said I, loud enough to be heard.

I was recompensed with a look of pensive gratitude. Every person present was emulous to express their sensibility and esteem, and my father declared to Algernon if he would promise faithfully to return, he would indulge him with leave to visit the 'man of nature and of truth.'

You may well conceive, my dear Charlotte, that there was nothing in this elegant and simple narration to check the prosecution of my design, and that I sought for the first favourable opportunity of disclosing my sentiments to my beloved Algernon. Indeed I judged it full time, for the grand catastrophe was advancing: a notification of my consent had been forwarded to England; preparations were making for the event, and Algernon, to avoid the sight of an exhibition he knew not how to prevent, was on the eve of returning home. Thinking myself justified by the tyranny of such circumstances to despise the ordinary rules of decorum, I resolved to consult with my Algernon. The result you shall have to-morrow.

CAROLINE.

LETTER XXXI.

HARD is the task, my Charlotte, to inspire you with disrespect for the woman who gave you birth; yet such may be your sentiment after reading this letter, But as you are so entwined in my heart, and so connected in my affairs, I cannot prevail on myself to conceal any thing from you, —not even the motives which impelled me to propose a measure to Algernon, and to act, in consequence, in a manner, that will, no doubt, in the eyes of the world, be deemed indecorous and reprehensible.

The world will exclaim against me for indelicacy and impatience; for not waiting till Algernon made a proposition which was to confirm the happiness of my life. The world knows nothing of Algernon, and appears equally ignorant of my sex. Sunk beneath me by birth and fortune, and soaring above me by pride of mind, Algernon could never consent to make me a proposal that might sully my reputation, or injure the high sense of honor he himself entertained.

And as to myself, the world should understand that women, when in love, are perhaps more passionately, more delicately sensible to the soft influence than men.—At least I can answer for myself, while under this sweet influence, I paid no manner of attention to the arguments of reason or of judgment.—What arguments, in fact, could be urged to a heart replete with so tender a passion? I gave way to imagination only, and to all the alarms that fancy could suggest. I was alive only to the pain of being torn from the object that was far dearer to me than myself. And these, my Charlotte, whatever the world may say to the contrary, these are the feelings—this the conduct of genuine love.

Woe to the woman whose heart is so little susceptible as to consult the little decorums of her sex, and the representations of interest, when she should be occupied in facilitating engagements that never can be too closely formed!

Woe to the waman who suffers a frigid indifference to preside over those engagements; and woe to the lovers whose passion is not equally ardent and reciprocal!

Believe me, Charlotte, in a mind uncorrupted by interest, love assumes the character, the noble pride of virtue; and it feels a degree of self-complacency—it glories in its transports.

Thus directed, I did not hesitate to seize the first opportunity of conversing with Algernon. This did not instantly occur: I lamented grievously the delay. The hours of suspense are years—are ages of torture to her who truly loves!—I at length met him reclined on his favourite seat near the old ruin in the garden. He rose up, bowed respectfully; endeavoured to suppress a rising sigh, and was about to retire.

The deepest sorrow was visible in his face.

'What, Algernon,' said I, 'do not 'you perceive that your Caroline is 'present? Ah! why, why would you 'fly? Why are you impatient to be 'gone?—Why do you look thus?'

"Madam," replied he, "it is my "duty to—it is my duty to retire; it is "my duty not to stop, not to express ———"

'What duty! why retire! why not 'expiess!' exclaimed I. 'Is my Al'gernon changed?—Has he no longer 'the same heart and mind? Does he 'cease to love his Caroline?—You sigh, 'my Algernon;—does your heart say 'that I must never be yours. Ha! you 'are speechless!—you are faint! sit 'down by your Caroline.'—He complied, and shortly recovered.

"Madam," said he, with a broken and faltering voice, "why all this good"ness to the unfortunate Algernon!—

" Why do you thus detain him? Be- " trothed as you are to the Marquis of " Albion, why do you not rather con- " jure him to be gone—conjure him to " die! Ah! would I were dead!— " would I were dead, rather than see you " in the arms of another; rather than see " myself condemned to wander through " the world, with a mind distracted, a " heart broken, a reason perturbed— " and no remedy, no hope, to cure such " dreadful affliction, or to mitigate such " poignant woes!"

'And do you think, Algernon,' said I, 'that were you dead; were you 'hopeless, were you unfortunate, that I 'should not be the victim of the most 'dreadful despair? Do you think,' repeated I, with a steady voice that seemed to issue from the centre of my soul, 'do you think that I should not 'also be devoured by the excess of 'your calamities! Do you think that 'a lingering if not a sudden death 'would not be my fate as well as yours. 'No, sir, I am not betrothed to the 'Marquis; my consent is only implied. 'Be assured then that I love you; that 'I love you with more ardour than 'ever, and that I will do every thing 'in my power to console you;—to 'confer upon you my fortune, my per-'son, and my heart—all that the most 'unbounded passion can desire!'

He was silent, but the duration of his silence was short.

"Bountiful providence," uttered he, with a look that made him appear lifted above the rest of mortals, "Bounti-"ful providence!"

But he could not proceed; and he fell on his knees by my side, clasping my hands with mingled transports of felicity and terror.

He again essayed to speak, but I know not what he said. I can only call to mind, that we alternately renewed a thousand protestations of everlasting love, that our hearts dwelt with transport on our intended felicity, and that we agreed to fly—with wings of love to fly, to the father of Algernon; to the "Man of Nature and of Truth," and, in his presence, and in the presence of that Being he reveres so much, from that holy bond which no human power could dare dissolve or dispute.

To the honor of Algernon it should be known, that, on the recovery of our serenity, he opposed every possible argument to the design. He spoke of his obligations to my father; mentioned my mother with tears of gratitude in his eyes; talked of dishonorable conduct; that it would prevent my marriage with the first subject in the B——— state, and bring upon himself a charge of venality of soul and interested designs.

'Cease, cease, my Algernon,' said I, 'my father has no right to dispose of 'my hand by violence; my mother 'will not be suspected privy to our at'tachment, and I call upon heaven 'to witness, that I will hereafter pub'licly declare, that I humbled myself 'before you; that it is I who injured 'the splendid reputation you have ac'quired; that it is I who protested 'against the match with the Marquis 'of Albion; and upon this princi'ciple, which I think a sufficient ex'cuse to every moderate and virtuous 'mind,—That I think the source of me'rit is not in birth, in rank, in riches, 'or in person, which are the capricious 'gifts of fortune, but in that virtue, 'goodness, and excellence, which are 'bestowed upon a favoured few, by an 'amiable, kind, and munificent Provi-'dence.'

The remainder of this interesting interview was occupied in the formation of such mechanical arrangements as promised success to an enterprize of so much importance and extent.

It was finally resolved that Algernon should, in the first instance, immediately repair to Ireland, there prepare for my reception ; attach some brave countrymen to his cause : then return by the way of Hamburgh, there hire a vessel for our speedy conveyance, and on his route to my father's court, from Hamburgh, plant relays of horses, and station his most trusty companions and friends.

Thus did every thing prophesy the happiest fruition to our views.—We returned, content and exulting to our society.

In a short time after Algernon procured leave to visit '*the man of nature and of truth;*' and I saw him depart with the blessings of our united family upon his head, and the innocence and the image of your mother, my Charlotte, engraven upon his heart. His farewell I shall never forget.

While saluting the Duke and Duchess, Melina, and Prince L——s, his mien was marked with dignity, grace, friendship, and gratitude, but as he approached to me, his mind was absorbed with but one sentiment of affection.

He took me by the hand; a lively colour glowed in his cheeks; his heart throbbed: he left the room with precipitation—as I must now conclude.

CAROLINE.

LETTER XXXII.

The langour occasioned by the absence of Algernon, my Charlotte, was occasionally interrupted and relieved, by the arrival of visitors to our court. As the most remarkable of these was the Reverend Doctor R———, Chaplain to the Marquiss of Albion, it would be doing injustice to him, were I not to take an early opportunity of introducing him in true colours to you and to the public.

Indeed this Reverened Divine is a most interesting subject to every speculative and philosophic character. His mind is not so much of a novel, as of an obsolete cast; for, from some strange combination of circumstances, some odd admixture of ingredients in his temperature, he seems capable of feeling no sentiment, of uttering no thought, but those which would have befitted a monkish polemic of three centuries back.—His very language and look partake of this complexion of mind: and one might know either from his diction or his countenance, that he was designed for some of those ages which are gone by, where the religious zealot evinced the purity of his faith by the austerity of his manners, and displayed the christian charity of his heart by intolerance and persecution.

Of the family from which this divine descended, no mention was made either in his introductory letters from the Countess of J——y, his friend, or in those of his patron, the Marquis. But from all I could learn, I have reason to think it is among the felicities of the Doctor, that his talents and his virtues are not obscured by the splendour of ancestry, and that his strong attachment to the dignities of his master, and to the ascendancy of power, cannot be attributed to early prejudices.

Sent to my father's court, as I soon understood from his conduct and manners, as a mere spy upon my life and habits, he omitted no occasion of obtaining intelligence, and at the same time of inculcating on the court, the virtues, the power, and the dignity of the House to which I was to be allied. —I must confess that I could not conceal from him the most sovereign contempt. When he railed against levity,

I have rose up and WALSED with Prince L——s, or any officer present, of my father's guards. When he declaimed against singing and music, I have taken my harp and run over the liveliest airs.

Whatever might have been the demerits of the Doctor, I soon found that I was wrong in the proceeding; I soon found that I should be the smarting victim of his hatred, and that I had inspired him with a brutal dislike towards me which would corrupt the happiness of my future days. However, notwithstanding his invincible antipathy to me, he paid me the most sycophantic attentions, and, although he appeared, so deservedly a monster to me, he was considered as an angel by my father, and by every other member of the court.—In short, his conversation, though stained with so much monastic jargon, was what is vulgarly called "Evangelical," and made him pass for a man endowed with all the virtues of the fathers of the primitive church.

I shall record, my Charlotte, for your amusement, perhaps for your instruction, what passed between the divine and your mother one Sunday morning, when he recommended me to substitute the Bible for the Poems of Pope which I held in my hand.

'Sir,' said I, 'I am reading the third 'part of the Essay on Man. Is there 'any thing immoral or vicious in that? '—For my part I cannot conceive any 'work more pious, more religious, 'more beautiful. How amiable a re'presentation of the Divine Being! a 'Being whose worship is love and gra-

'titude! whose service is a state of 'manly and rational freedom! whose 'sovernignty over us is but a more 'enlarged power to do us good—A 'God whose proper character is that 'most endearing one of Father!— 'What a noble assemblage of tender 'and affecting ideas, does this poem 'inspire!—How different from the 'too usual representations of church-'men and priests!—By your general 'way of thinking, Sir,' continued I, animated by the remembrance of my Algernon,—'one would be tempted 'to believe in a wicked diety at 'the helm of things, instead of a 'kind and benevolent principle.— 'Surely you make an improper use 'of the Holy Bible. You do not 'describe the Almighty, as the poem 'does, as a Being who diffuses 'around us the kindly influences of 'love and beauty, but you prefer to 'paint him to our affrighted imagi-'nations, with all the pomp and 'terror of dreadful and austere ma-'jesty; a kind of omnipotent tyrant 'at the head of an universe of slaves; 'who accordingly must pay their 'court to him, if they hope to es-'cape his vengeance, or enjoy any 'thing of his favor, and that by ab-'ject servility, mean adulation, and 'forced reverence. Yet, Sir, the lan-'guage of this Essay, of unpreju-'diced reason and nature; the lan-'guage of the Scriptures themselves, 'speaks quite other things of a su-'preme Director. And we find, as 'Pope here observes, "a Sovereign 'Being, and a sovereign Good," 'are equivalent expressions. Indeed 'the two ideas are too intimately 'allied to each other, that it asto-

‘ nishes me how you can pretend to ‘ separate them. For what thoughts ‘ can you entertain of the great Au- ‘ thor of blessings, but that he must ‘ be in himself a Being of the most ‘ perfect benevolence.

‘ Suffer me then, Sir,’ continued I,—‘ to pursue my devotion after ‘ my own way, and do you be well ‘ assured, that if you came to this ‘ court for the purpose of compel- ‘ ling innocence to yield to oppres- ‘ sion, and of making me a victim ‘ to the interests of your master, or ‘ to the arbitrary laws of your na- ‘ tion, a knowledge of the true God ‘ is a stranger to your religion, and ‘ your Bible and the rites of your ‘ church have not contributed to the ‘ humanity or to the illumination of ‘ your character.’

He bit his lips, appeared confused, and retired. I was again culpable. Such conduct could not serve to mitigate the resentment he already entertained for the unfortunate and devoted

CAROLINE.

LETTER XXXIII.

My soul turns with disgust, my sweet girl, from such a man as I described to you in my last, and allows my mind to dwell with delight on a being of contrasted principles, manners and affections.

What! on Algernon? No—On whom then? On a brother, on a beloved brother, who had been absent so considerable a time, that I scarcely indulged a hope of seeing him again, and have since seen so little of him, that I have hitherto found no occasion to mention him to you in this series of letters. His birth, his rank in life, and his relationship to you, however, render it necessary that I should detail all the particulars of his history; and I assure you, the task of describing a young warrior, affords me more pleasure than what I derived from my late description of a monk of the last, or rather, of the present century.

Descended as my brother was, from the first blood in Germany, you may well conceive that nothing was omitted that might render him an ornament to his rank; and I am proud to tell you, that the toward genius of the boy, amply rewarded the attention that had been bestowed upon it. The Duke, his father, cherished the thought that his son would uphold the dignity of his House, nor suffer a stain to rest on its bright honor; and in the field he nothing questioned but that he would earn a name great as his ancestors; for the boy delighted in the use of arms;

and he soon became distinguished for the skill and readiness with which he handled them. At exercises, among a crowd of contending nobles, he ever shone conspicuous, as much by his dignified air, and manly graceful form, as by the number and splendour of his train, which my father enabled him to support. In the diversions, the strength and vigour of his arm in using the lance, or the sword, the firmness with which he maintained his saddle, and the dexterity he shewed in triumphing over his opponents, met the praise and admiration of all. And while his skill gained him the applause of the public, his success never filled him with arrogance or pride.

From trying his arms in many bloodless encounters, particularly with my beloved Algernon, who was the companion of his youth, he ardently longed to signalize himself in the field of battle. The talk of the Duke, which mostly turned upon war, served to inflame this desire. And when war was the discourse, he would dwell on the theme with never-tired attention. By the hour he would sit and listen to his father while he spoke of the martial feats he had done in his youth, or described the figure of the battles he had been in, and how they had been won or lost. When of these matters he spoke, the boy's eyes would flash with unwonted fire, and a martial ardour would animate his whole frame. Then did the roused spirit of war, restless and impatient of an idle life, strike some of its fire into his words.

'Oh, Father!' exclaimed he, 'would 'it were my fortune to tread in the 'steps of my ancestors, who oft-times 'fought from morn till even'; and all 'stained and red with the blood of 'warriors, sought out glory even in 'the jaws of death itself, till covered 'with wounds they fell gloriously in 'the field of battle! Oh, that such a 'fate was mine! Better so to perish 'than live an hundred years in vulgar 'indolence and ignominious ease!'

"Thou little thinkest boy," replied his father, in order to prove him, "on "the hardships that to a soldier's life "are familiar. Patient of heat and cold, "of hunger and thirst, the soldier must "endure the long and toilsome march, "and the battle's rage. At night, when "the combat's finished, he throws his "limbs, stiff with wounds, and all "smeared with blood, upon the bare "earth, perchance, and in the midst "of tumult, snatches a short repose "till the morrow's sun awakes him to "fresh fatigues and dangers. Oh, my

" boy! will it not shake thee from thy " manhood, when the fate of war rives " from thee some faithful friend, and " thou beholdest thy fellow-soldiers fall " in heaps around thee, who, perhaps, " a minute before were exulting in the " pride of victory? The stroke of death " comes, and their lifeless, bleeding " bodies strew the field! When thou " findest difficulties and dangers in- " crease: hemmed in and close pressed " by the enemy; no succour nigh; sink- " ing with famine and fatigue; the war- " worn soldier stretched on the earth " in the open air; no couch but the " ground—he enjoys a short respite " from misery, till the beating of the " hollow drum, and the shrill sound of " the trumpet calls him to resist the " midnight attack; when, I say, thou " encounterest all these things as thy " father lately did in the detested plains " of Champaigne, and on his route to

"Paris to preserve the tottering House "of Bourbon, wilt thou not wish, my "boy, thou never hadst engaged in "war? Speak! Now speak!"

'Oh, my father!' cried the youth, 'what are hardships to a mind intent on 'fame? What are dangers to him who 'aims at glory? They but serve as 'goads to urge him forward. It is no- 'thing to meet the perils you speak 'of. By Heaven! I'd fain encounter 'them all; and as I endured the ut- 'most dangers of a soldier's life, I'd 'think I was enjoying a life of peace. 'Be honor my guide. And if I pe- 'rish, mine will be no coward's death. 'My sword shall carve me out a monu- 'ment; and when I am found surround- 'ed by the dead bodies of my enemies, 'lifeless and bleeding, men shall say— 'He perished nobly!'

" Thy ardent spirit delights my " heart!" said the Duke, " not one of " our House but hath earned a name " in the field. I have early marked thy " valorous spirit, and I doubt not but " thou wilt prove thyself worthy of " thy race. Go, my noble boy, give " thy fire vent, and tread the rugged " path of fame. Haste thee to Berlin, " and learn to fight for thy God, thy " religion, and thy king. Haply thy " sovereign may renew the war. Hap- " ly thou mayest enter France, and re- " deem the fame thy father lost. Hap- " ly thou mayest drive the fainting " French like dust before the wind. " Famine and treachery alone caused " me to yield. Would the time were " again! But my arm has no more its " former strength. It shall recover it, " my son, for you shall share with me " the glory of the field: the time per- " haps may come. Under thy father

" thou canst at least be formed to fight
" —though not perhaps to conquer."

'My Lord! my father!' exclaimed the young Prince, 'shall I then to the 'field? My soul is fired, and eager for 'the combat! And shall I hear the 'glorious din of battle! Oh, let the 'time come fast, when the trumpets 'clang calls me to the field of glory! 'Heavens! what a glorious moment 'will that be! Methinks, I see the 'armour of the embattled hosts gleam-'ing in the sun, and hear the full-toned 'voice of my father encouraging his 'soldiers. The instruments of war 'sound a charge, and the warriors rush 'to the battle! My father at the head 'of his troops; and as he waves his 'glittering falchion over his head, 'cries,' " Follow, my son, follow me."

" Thy words give happy presage," said the Duke, " that thou wilt not de-" generate from thy valiant forefathers, " who often fought and bled for their " country and their God. May the " spirit that glowed in their bosoms, " and nobly urged them on to deeds of " valour, reign in thine: and may'st " thou, like them, carry death and vic-" tory on thy sword's point. When in " the hour of battle thou strikest, let " the love of glory move thy arm; and " thy courage and fury in the fight be " only equalled by thy clemency to " those who yield: then hear the voice " of mercy plead to stay the uplifted " sword from further slaughter! Re-" member that courage not more be-" cometh a soldier than humanity. " Double is his victory, that saves " from death the unresisting foe! Be-" ware of that wild impetuosity which " often hurries thee beyond prudence:

"trust me, boy, 'twill lead thee else "to nought but to destruction. May "the Almighty God, whose battles "thou may'st have to fight against in- "fidel France, preserve thy life; that "I may oft' fight with thee. But if "the end of life should come ere that, "I am content, so I hear thou dost "honor to thy name and country!"

Soon after this interesting dialogue, my brother departed for Berlin; he soon distinguished himself both in the camp and in the court; rapidly rose to the rank of Colonel and Aid de Camp to the king, and returned to us on leave of absence, one of the bravest and most accomplished of men. My father and he were inseparable, and he had more than ever attached himself to me, by lamenting the absence of my adored Algernon.

In short, who did not lament his absence? Poor Melina, though she conquered in her breast every idea of personal attachment, had not yet learned to live without his presence, and Prince L——s, whose passion for her is tempered into a brotherly affection, talked to her in the kindest manner both of the esteem which Algernon entertains for her, and of his speedy return. However, were it not for my brother, the animated, lively young warrior, I doubt much but we should compose a dull set —a group rather of still than of animatedlife. He it is, to whom we are indebted for the mitigation of the pain of Algernon's absence, and of the dull society to which a court is so often condemned. At this time, too, the arrival of other English visitors was expected. Lady and Sir William H——, I heard named by the Rev. Doctor R——. I may sketch their character in my next.

CAROLINE.

LETTER XXXIV.

When I introduced the Reverend Doctor R—— to your notice, my dear child, I might have omitted to mention, that it is also among the felicities of his life, that his religion is of so accommodating a nature as to justify the most shameful adulation and flattery of his patrons, and the most malicious and intemperate representation of the rest of mankind. But you shall judge; the H——n's arrived: 'tis to the Doctor's history of them I am indebted for the matter of which I intend this letter shall be composed.

There is no country, it would seem from the Doctor's account, where the rank that women ought to hold in the scale of the creation, is so disputed as in England. Some of the English are of opinion, that women may be taught their letters, but should never learn their mischievous combinations; others, of a softer mould, have in a manner depressed while they exalted them, by bursting forth into rapturous eulogies on their amiable virtues, which they would at the same time confine to the kitchen and nursery; while a third sort, with more liberality than the one, and more boldness than the other, contend that literature alone exalts the female character, and that every step a woman mounts in the ladder of erudition, makes her more eminent in excellence:

" Victor que verum volitare per ora."

Among the votaries of the third sect, I am instructed, my Charlotte, by the

Reverend Divine, to enrol the name of Sir William H———n. He began life with a determination to run counter to the rest of the world; not even to exist on the surface of that world, but to excavate its womb and reside in the subterraneous cities of Herculaneum and Pompeia. But above all, his determination was to oppose the long established usage of mankind, in the choice of a wife. For he sighed when he reflected on the slavish subjection in which man detains his injured helpmate, in defiance of reason and in contempt of humanity; he burnt with all the zeal of an enthusiast to fight the battles of this last and fairest work of nature, and resolved to shew the world that he felt what he expressed, by drawing some deserving female from humble life; by providing her with books in all the learned languages, superintending her education with scrupulous anxiety, and at a fit period leading her to the altar, crowned with never fading flowers of science and learning. This philanthropic scheme, he immediately put into the happiest execution.

Sir William was a member of the Royal Society, and Society of Painting, Sculpture, and Arts, &c. at Somerset-House. To this house of miscellaneous fame, he had been accustomed to see a lovely girl arrive twice a week in the season, and hire herself to the students as a model for the naked figures they intended to draw a Medician Venus of the first order of beauty, and for which the society proposed to grant the highest honors and pecuniary rewards. The arrival of this sweet girl, did not appear very extraordinary to Sir William, because it was customary for the society to select the finest women of the streets for this species of exhibition, nor did he take considerable notice of her till he discovered that she had been bred a milk-maid in the most obscure shades of ignorance, and yet, that on coming on the town, she lent her person to the society, with a degree of ardour that evinced the delight she took in the diffusion and improvement of the arts. This pleased Sir William; it seemed an earnest of future literary greatness, and immediately determined him to gain some personal acquaintance with the damsel, in order to find whether at some future period she was likely to answer his matrimonial views. In a few days he discovered her abode, offered his protection, and had the satisfaction to find that she expressed an entire readiness to submit to his commands and to his instruction. They accordingly departed hand in hand. The lovely Fanny, for so she was called, immediately entered upon her course of lectures, with an alacrity that both surprized and gratified her protector. She learned to read even quicker than Madame de Genlis' infant Prodigies; soon became acquainted with a large portion of English literature; and in the course of a few years was mistress of music and drawing; and of the French, Italian, Spanish and German languages.

He now considered the time as having arrived, which fate had fixed for his marriage. Fanny could make no objection; a licence was obtained, and Sir William and his lovely Fanny were introduced to the public as man and wife. His pleasures did not, like that of many others, end with the honeymoon, but received a daily accession of light; for surely no woman, since the days of divine Etherida, was ever possessed of such rare and valuable virtues. The common failings of common women were unknown to Lady H——n; her lofty mind towered above her sex, and displayed such a collection of singular endowments, that Sir William took her to the Continent, where she was considered the most accomplished and adorable of her sex. At Naples, where she long resided, she was considered a blaze of beauty and excellence, and it is said, that the King of ——! But, my dear Charlotte, it would be ungenerous in me to pursue the Rev. Doctor's account. It would shock your feelings, and revolt my mind. He is a base calumniator. Lady H——n is a charming, and I believe a virtuous wife. She has been in my company. Take my opinion of her—the above remarks proceed, as I observed, from the Doctor's satirical account.

When woman passes through that thorny path of pleasure—foreign courts, without being drawn astray by the temptations, which perpetually assail the innocent; our esteem and veneration ought ever to await her. Among such, Lady H——n certainly claims pre-eminence from her splendid endowments of mind, joined to an unspotted fame; for I pay no regard to the calumny of such a man as Doctor R——, or to any-thing that is said by the reptiles who bask in the sunshine of a court. It is natural for envy and malice to persecute beauty and worth; and to these alone I attribute the attacks made on her at Naples, and elsewhere.

As to the rest, nature has bestowed on Lady H———n, a magistic person, a striking lovely countenance, and a fine melodious voice; the judgment with which she modulates the last of these, has never been excelled, perhaps never rivalled, by any private speaker or singer. The flexibility of her features, the expression of her eyes, and the grace of her deportment, have seldom been equalled. We were all delighted with her society, and lamented exceedingly, when Sir William announced his intention of returning to Naples, where he was destined to remain as envoy of his king. During her residence with us, she frequently conversed with me on the subject of my intended marriage with the Marquis of Albion; whom she represented as one of the most elegant, accomplished, and amiable of men; but finding that this rather excited a painful sensibility than an expected pleasure, she dropt such discourses, and took up topics unconnected with the wanderings of the heart, or the delicacy of the mind. Indeed the time was approaching when I expected the return of my Algernon, and this hope occupied and absorbed the whole of my thoughts. I had received a letter from him, stating, that every thing had succeeded to his warmest wish: that his friends lent their aid to all his desires, and that he was about to return and secure the hand of his Caroline, or perish in the attempt. Ha! "or perish in the attempt!" My Charlotte, even now this dereadful idea disturbs me. I cannot proceed.

Adieu,

CAROLINE.

LETTER XXXV.

At the moment I was deploring the most, my temporary separation from Algernon, and looking forward with the utmost anxiety to the hour which should restore him to my arms, I received a letter from him, stating, that he was on the eve of embarkation, and hoped soon to behold her who was dearer to him than the rest of the world beside.

Several weeks elapsed, my Charlotte, and no Algernon arrived!—What a painful interval to one possessing so fond, so undisguised a heart; so timid, and yet so ardent an affection!—Every gale which blew, raised a storm, far more violent in my breast.—Nor was sleep attended with its usual repose, One horrible vision in particular, deserves to be perpetually recorded. I dreamt that my residence was within view of the sea, and that during the raging of a violent tempest, a vessel in distress hove in sight; and soon after bilged, and was entirely wrecked.—I hurried down to the shore, in a state little short of frenzy. I thought I heard the voice, the faltering fainting voice of my Algernon!—Overpowered by this terrible impression, I precipitated myself from an elevated part of the shore into the waves. Then, methought the faithful Algernon saved me from being entirely engulphed, though being himself in a state almost lifeless. I woke. But so much had the shock affected my imagination and mental powers, that I started wildly from my bed, nor could for a time convince myself that I had not seen him perish with my own eyes.

In a short time after, however, I received a letter renewing a thousand protestations of everlasting love; dwelling with transport on approaching felicity, and fixing the day, the hour, and the place, where I was to meet my Algernon!

It may be supposed that in proportion to the pleasure, the delight I derived from this intelligence, I anticipated the happy concurrences, and that I was at the place where my lover was to alight, even some time before I could expect his arrival. My eye was continually at the window. At the least noise 'it is he! it is he!' I exclaimed. The moment horsemen appeared I was the first to perceive them.

I had wings—I flew—with impatient eyes I sought my beloved

'Where is he? where is he? Is not 'my Algernon with you?' said I to a gentleman that approached me with a character of sorrow visible in his face.

"Madam," said he, "it is my pro-"vince to———"

'What!' interrupted I, 'is he not 'come, Sir?—he told me—he wrote 'me word—do, say what prevents him?

"I am his friend, Madam, and I am "come express," replied the gentleman.

'What!' reiterated I again,—'What, 'Sir, has he changed his mind—does 'he cease to love me?—Does he re-'pent?—Does his father refuse?—Is 'he intimidated by danger?—Is he no

'longer the same?—You sigh, Sir;—'
'must I then never be his?—Speak,
'Sir!—tell me!'

"Oh! Madam," returned the noble stranger, "excuse that anxiety that "makes me tremble: but do not be-"lieve that my friend is capable of cow-"ardly or dishonorable conduct—but ———"

'Ah! he is sick,' cried I, 'I run, I 'fly—to succour, to behold him.'

At these words the stranger regarded me with a look of the most extreme sensibility. I was nearly speechless and immoveable.—'Ah, Sir, I under-'stand you too well,' I at length exclaimed, 'he is dead! he is dead!'

"Good God! Madam," interrupted he hastily, "no, Heavens forbid he "should be dead! Heavens forbid "your fears should be well founded! "No, your Algernon lives; and lives "to love you with more ardour than "ever; but I, his friend, would not "allow him to approach your fa-"ther's capital. It might lead to a "discovery of his intentions. I have "compelled him to wait disguised a "few leagues distance. Here is the "letter entreating you to arrange "your flight, and then to repair with "me to the place where you both "shall meet, never, it is hoped, to be "separated more. Prepare then, "Madam," pursued he, "prepare "without delay;—your passion, I per-"ceive is equally ardent and recipro-"cal—may Providence preserve it "from interruption!"

You may well be convinced, my Charlotte, that I suggested no difficulty;

that I did not delay a moment to fly on the wings of love to my adorable Algernon: that I was impatient to commence a journey which was to confirm the happiness of my life, and that I thought life itself attached to those ties of marriage which can never be too closely united.

Having entered into the particulars of my retreat, with the interesting stranger, and formed a plan the most likely to be attended with success, I returned to the palace, and there abandoned myself to the government of the most severe and poignant emotions.

The instant I saw my mother, my mind began to fill with agonizing penitence; and when I beheld my father, whose views of ambition and happiness I was about to frustrate, I thought my heart would break for bringing him to the grave with sorrow and dissappointment. In short, all was confusion within my breast: every thing tended to bewilder my imagination, and to induce me at the same time, to sacrifice all the moral obligations of the mind.

I was not, however, ignorant how long and how happily I enjoyed the sunshine of parental tenderness, but the recollection of its beams could cheer me no longer; I was insensible to every warmth but what emanated from my Algernon's love, and considered no obligation so binding as the promise I had made of uniting myself to him for life.

And is it to be wondered at that I entertained for him so sincere, so sacred an affection? He was educated with a brother tenderly belove'd. I saw the youth, under my father's protection, increase in stature and in knowledge. I saw him most loved and most praised. He stood high in the world's estimation. I was satisfied that to none more deserving could I render so dear a gift as my heart—and dear it was to my Algernon. He had placed his affections upon me long before he dared to hope for my concurrence. Nor had he long to plead; I soon confessed with virgin hesitation, while the blush of timid modesty mantled in crimson hue upon my cheek, that my heart was his, and that the nuptial tie, in spite of destiny, should join our hands, as love had united our hearts.

But why do I weary you with reflections? Rather let me hasten to inform you, that I made every necessary arrangement for my flight, and appointed the hour, &c. in which I should confide myself to the escort of L—d E—d F— G——d, who was the friend introduced to me for this purpose by my beloved Algernon.—Too much exhausted to enter into such interesting particulars at the close of so long a letter, I must turn your attention to the next communication of

CAROLINE.

LETTER XXXVI.

In compliance with the arrangements I had entered into with L—d E——d F— G———d, I abandoned the place of my birth and the graves of my father, and met him at the time and situation previously marked out. Oppressed as I then was with a thousand terrors, I was in no state to mark aught that passed. The clock had just struck midnight, and clinging in speechless agitation to my fearless deliverer, I trembled in silence for the moment that I should behold my Algernon and breathe a more vivifying air.

Never! my Charlotte, never! no never, shall I forget that instant when

I passed the last door that surrendered me to liberty. Though my heart bounded with joy, yet every limb trembled, as with an ague, and I hung heavy on the arm of L—d E——d, whose unshaken nerves and dauntless mien showed that his soul felt none of that terror which appalled mine.—With one hand he supported me, with the other he grasped his sword.

In this manner we reached a house where I was to assume the garb of an English youth, and then proceed on horseback to the concealment of my lover. Scarce could I maintain my seat so much did the appearances of every thing, and the reverberation of every sound, threaten and terrify me. How quick throbbed my bosom, when I found myself without the view of the palace; but the sense of danger I knew not yet to encounter, and the agonizing apprehensions my fancy framed, damped, or blotted every joy ; and to augment the bitter ingredients of my cup, I soon understood that the place of my Algernon's retreat, was more distant than I was given to comprehend. We reached it, however, by sun-rise, but would have gained it much sooner had not L—d E——d deemed it prudent to take a circuitous forest path in preference to the more frequented and public road.

Sick at heart with fear, I had sunk to the earth on alighting from my horse; but Algernon came to my support, and with a dear embrace, in honied words poured the soothing balm of hope, which, like aliment to those that perish, restored a portion of my wasted strength, and cheered my drooping spirits. The state of anxious terror in which I was began to subside, and after a hasty repast and two hours repose, I took a new and renovated departure.

After some time of uninterrupted travel, Algernon pointed out to me at a distance, a hill on which stood a temple where he intended to make his first halt. Adorned with columns of resplendent white marble, it rose from the bosom of a laurel grove, toward the azure vault of Heaven ; beyond the grove the view was lost in the wide expanse of æther. It was mid-day. The sand was scorching hot, and the sun darted his rays so directly on our heads, that the shadows of the locks of hair, which covered our foreheads, extended over the whole face. The panting reptile dragged himself with pain among the ferns that bordered our path. Our people preserved a dead silence. No sound was heard, save that of the grasshopper chirping amidst the meadow's springing herbs. At each step there rose a cloud of dust to inflame the eyes and parch the lips.

Thus we labored on, oppressed by fear and languor; but soon increased our pace when we saw before us on the border of our path some high and spreading trees. This shade was dark as night. Seized with pious gratitude and awe, we entered the grove, and there inhaled a most refreshing breeze. This delicious place afforded, at once, all that could flatter every sense. The tufted trees enclosed a verdant spot, watered by a pure and gelid stream. The branching shadows of the trees trembled in the channel; and the wild rose, jessamine, and mulberry, twined in rich clusters round their trunks. A bubbling spring rose from the foot of a monument, surrounded by honey-suckles, the sickly willow, and the creeping ivy. 'O God! my Algernon!' I cried, 'how enchanting is this place! my soul 'venerates the beneficent hand that 'planted these delightful shades. His 'ashes here, perhaps repose. See those 'characters that appear through the 'branches of the honey-suckle on the 'front of the tomb. They perhaps 'may tell us who it was vouchsafed 'this solace for the weary traveller. On 'saying these words, I turned aside 'the branches and read as follows—'

"Here rest the ashes of a Hasburgh, whose life was one continued series of boundless glory and bounteous deeds."

'The tomb of my grandfather!' exclaimed I, 'Oh! my Algernon! this 'is too much to bear. I remember he 'loved me with the tenderest solicitude: 'I was filled with veneration for his 'very name: must I! ah, must I! be-

'fore the evening sun, turn my back 'upon his grave, and leave his wretch'ed descendant to shed unavailing tears 'for the conduct of a Hasburgh and a 'daughter?'—I was faint. "Rest your"self, my Caroline,' said Algernon, "rest yourself beneath these cooling "shades."—He sat down by me, after looking a long time at me, with a gracious smile, yet with eyes in which the tear trembled, he continued:

"Caroline, my love, your candour, "your cares, your sensibility, all, all "delight me. Believe me, I, too, "honor the memory of thy parents. "Your mother is full of benevolence "and virtue. Your father is the first "general of the age; and this tomb "contains the ashes of a man, amiable "and beneficent, magnanimious and "grand—may his posterity be for ever "blessed!—But what do I say? Am

" I not calling down curses upon that " posterity? am I not the instrument " of its degradation and disgrace? Ca- " roline! why did I love thee? Born " in indigence, why did I aspire to the " hand of a Princess?"

His voice faltered, my hand fell from his; he was about to rise. I trembled, blushed—yet detained him by my side. He again took my hand, and again his voice died upon his lips. My head reclined on his breast which I bedewed with tears.

' Oh Algernon,' said I, ' forgive your ' Caroline! She loves you, but the idea ' of never again walking beneath these ' shades, or of beholding the blessed ' tomb they protect, made her neglect ' her lover, and pour forth all the sor- ' rows of her heart. Precious relics, 'pleasing shades, transparent fountain,' exclaimed I, 'Farewell! farewell!'

On this repetition Algernon and I rose as if directed by one sudden impulse, and filled with the divine sensations of love, piety, and gratitude, we directed our steps to where L—d E—d had more than once invited us to partake of the rural repast which he had prepared with all the attentions and solicitude which distinguished the disinterested friend.—Excuse this abrupt close—I am too weary to proceed.

CAROLINE.

LETTER XXXVII.

The rose of the spring of life and health having been restored to my cheek by the refreshment and repose which I derived from my stay in the grove of the temple, we prepared to travel under the sable veil of night; and left the delicious retreat with hearts occupied by various and contending sensations. Tears of sympathy and tenderness bedewed my cheek.—Algernon perceived them. "You weep, my Caroline," he said, fixing his eyes tenderly upon me. "What is there in your heart that can make them flow?"

I wiped the drops from my cheeks, but my eyes still filled with fresh tears, and I turned them back to the tomb of my grandfather. Algernon understood the appeal, and I could read in his countenance that his mind was as much affected as if I had uttered volumes.

"There is no pain my Caroline," said he, after a pause eminently expressive, "but what we can diminish by "the contemplation of our hopes and "of our affections, nor is there any "pleasure can equal that we feel after "performing the sacred rites which "are destined to unite us. The bright "radiance of the morn; the mellowed "light of the setting sun, the moon "that now pierces through the obscu-"rity of the night, the grave which you "abandon, the country to which you "belong, the parents to whom you "owe your birth, all fill the heart with "delicious sensations. But that, which

" love inspires—O, my Caroline, it is " far, far more delicious!"

Alas! my child, it is unnecessary to tell you that my heart assented to all he said; it began to pant in my bosom, though it caused the words to hang upon my lips.

In this manner we continued to pursue the early part of our nocturnal journey. Algernon riding close to my side, and L—d E——d attending to the conduct and security of his friends and party: the whole being led by a trusty guide, who professed to know the passes and defiles of the mountainous country through which prudence directed us to pursue the principal part of the remainder of our way. But Night's dusky shadows had for a few hours only spread over the face of the earth, when we had the mortification to discover the fallibility of our guide. In short, the sun had not long hid its lustre behind the western hills, before we lost our road, and had to make our way between craggy hollow places, rugged rocks and narrow shelves, or to mount up the steep acclivities of those mountainous regions which form the north-west boundary of my father's extensive domains.

In a march so toilsome and tedious, our progress was perpetually retarded by almost inaccessible declivities and rocky ledges, scarce rendering space or foot-hold to our horses. Slow and cautious as is the sluggish snail in its movements, we proceeded onward. Sometimes a huge precipitous cliff opposed a vast front, and denied an avenue; at other times immense chasms of prodigious depth, present themselves to the affrighted sight. Which ever way we turned, difficulties innumerous still sprung up; and, as soon as one obstacle was surmounted, another appeared to exercise the patience or to appal the mind.

Faint, and exhausted with unavailing labour and solicitude, we agreed to halt for the night. The party agreed to this welcome order, with heart-felt alacrity, and stretched their weary length under the shelter of the hanging rock.

Seated on a projecting eminence, Algernon and I endeavoured to mitigate the sense of our situation, and to avert the apprehensions of further calamity. Fortunately for us, as we rested the moon shone with the utmost splendor, and afforded us light to view the wild beauty of the prospect. It was closed on every side with rugged precipices of dark and forlorn hue, broken into vast chasms; dark cliffs, whose shelving pinnacles were clothed with many tall pines; and projecting crags, shagged with bushes and brambles, and terrible with the remains of decayed trees blasted by the lightning of the Heavens!

From the midst of these precipices appeared an impetuous torrent dashing over broken rocks from one precipice to another: foaming, it swiftly dartcd over its precipitous channel, alternately appearing and disappearing as it wound its rapid course among the rocks; some, whose bleak brows were wholly bare, and some, whose every hollow and crag was thickly covered with the lucid heath and grey furze.

It was, my Charlotte, the still and lonely hour of midnight, and not a sound, save the distant and continual murmurs of the torrent, as it fell from rock to rock, reverberating the sound in the hollows of the worn cliffs, through which its unwearied wave, beating perpetually, had formed a passage, disturbed the general silence. The wind was hushed into a gentle breeze, which sighed amid the leaves of the lofty pines that grew up the craggy mountain's sides. The moon rode high in the vault of Heaven; its lustre shining on the grey rocks, and dancing on the rushing waters, added to the wild romantic appearance of the place. Its unbroken solitude and lonely situation inspired a solemn awe, and rendered the circumstances under which we were placed at once terrific and interesting.

Wearied, however, with the extreme toil which I endured since my flight from the palace, and somewhat soothed by the reviving conversation of my beloved Algernon, I gradually sunk upon his breast, and without slumbering enjoyed the repose of slumber.

While I was in this state, Algernon kept anxiously awake, and thinking me insensible in sleep, uttered over me, in a low voice, the following numbers which merit perpetually to be remembered.

"May thy slumbers be tranquil, O my Caroline! and refreshing as the morning breeze. Rest gently on my bosom, as the drops of dew repose upon the leaves of the lily, when the breath of morn agitates the flowers. How soft, how sweet are the slumbers of innocence!

"Descend from Heaven sweet dreams! You that attend the lovely train of sports and mirth, descend on Cynthia's rays, and hover round my Caroline. Present to her mind nought but smiling plains, green pastures, peace and content in the simple cottage of her Algernon!

"Let her think she hears a concert of the sweetest flutes, resounding in the lovely valley of my father. Or, may she seem to bathe in his limpid stream, beneath the shade of jessamines and woodbine which I planted, and where she can be beheld by none, except the birds that fly from tree to tree, and sing for her alone!

"Lovely dreams! conduct her to the groves on Shannon's banks, where flowers are interwoven with perpetual verdure. There, let the little loves pursue and play around her, as bees about the new-blown rose. Let one present her with fruit, another with flowers, while some of the lovely group wave garlands with their wings, and diffuse around her the sweetest odours.

" Within the grove let the God of Love appear; but without his arrow or his quiver; lest he alarm her timid innocence. Let him be adorned only with the charms of his enchanting youth. Let her seem to sport with his graces: let her call him her companion and her brother, and fear not to reveal to him her love for her Algernon!

" Yes, sweet dreams, deign at last to present to her my image. Let her see me languish at her feet, and with down-cast eyes, say, in flattering accents, that for her I live—that for her I die. Ah! at this dream, may a sigh heave her bosom! may she then blush and smile upon me."

He had no sooner concluded his beautiful apostrophe, than I destroyed the sweet delusion by shewing that I was awake, and by exclaiming

" Sweeter thy song, Algernon! than the rill
" Which rolls its music down this rocky hill."

'I have heard your words,—they are sweet as honey from the lips distilled.'

The moon brightened my countenance, he saw that I regarded him with a gentle smile; he saw a vivid blush glow upon my cheek. He press- me with ardour to his breast. I felt confused. A wild and sudden affright visited all my senses. I grew pale; withdrew from his arms; shunned his looks; his eyes seemed to brighten with doubtful joys; the posture, the place, the youth, all served to confirm my fears;—opprest with shame, with downcast looks, and silent anguish streaming down my face, I had only power to say, O, Algernon! leave me, leave me. Be not false to thy vows, a traitor to thy flame! Respect the innocence of the unfortunate Caroline!'

With what pitying attention did he hear me speak! With what melting inspiration did he touch my heart! With what sweet persuasion did he infuse the balm of hope and confidence into my alarmed breast! With what delicacy did he remove my fears! With what solicitude did he again invite me to repose in his protecting arms!

Encouraged by a conviction of his integrity, and occupied only with the pleasures of a guiltless love, I made no shew of affected resistance; but, wearied with toil and contending sensations, committed myself to his protection, and in a short time fell to rest upon his honorable though heaving breast.

But repose was denied me! I was haunted by unpleasant dreams, and frightful visions! Algernon watched me like a guardian angel—he soothed me as I started, he wiped away the tears that bedewed my cheeks—my broken sighs awakened all his fears, he felt I was unhappy—his limbs trembled with their burthen—I awoke.

Oh! my Charlotte, the refined and virtuous passion we entertained for each other, deserved—not condemnation, but applause. It was a primitive love; a dignified tenderness; an affection natural to honest minds; such as was held in esteem in this country, before the British gallantry lost its genuine lustre and innocence, in the dissolute manners of a neighbouring nation; which has, unfortunately, succeeded in the corruption of its pleasures, morals, and politics.

And it is so very rare to find, amongst the people of fashion in England, a pair, who have any true relish for the elegant delights of a chaste, mutual and disinterested love, that I question much whether the passion which existed between Algernon and me, will be credited. Ever since the generality of the men are turned libertines, and the most part of women coquettes, genuine love is, in a manner, banished out of life; and marriage is, in effect, only a mere legal contract to live at variance under the same roof.

But, let the world enjoy its opinion! Be that as it may, I continue to state to you all the particulars of my extraordinary flight, and I shall only observe, that I would not for worlds, be that person who can neither believe nor enjoy the narrative. But it is now late, and I am so wearied by this long letter, that it must content you to know, that as Algernon and I resumed our serenity, we passed the remainder of the night in the softest manner; in whispering the tenderest things; in making the most engaging vows, and in swearing the most unalterable fidelity: perhaps, too, in saying what prudent women might deem dangerous, and what vicious women would not have honestly to avow, or confidence to reveal. That is, I told my Algernon that I loved him; that I should never love any but him; that I indulged my heart in no pleasure, but the fond idea of becoming his wife, of reposing upon his breast, and revealing to him every latent merit I might discover in his character. Adieu, my child, for the present.

CAROLINE.

LETTER XXXVIII.

Amusing the hours, my Charlotte, in the manner described to you in my last, and admiring at the same time the wild beauties of nature in the desolate country where we reposed, Algernon started; and bending forward, thought he perceived the deficient light of the night supplied by an artificial illumination in a distant part of the route we had traversed the preceding day.

Alas! his conjecture was but too correct; the darkness of the valley was dispersed by the bright blaze of torches, and voices were heard, and people discovered as if searching about the rocks, and looking for some persons, or for some object with a more than ordinary degree of impatience and solicitude.

With the fervid intellect and inventive genius of a woman, I considered these appearances as supernatural. In proportion as this idea, excited by the sublimity of the refracted lights, and reverberation of voices, gained upon me, I was the more distant from the true knowledge of the danger which threatened to pursue me. I thought of nothing but of apparitions; and as the light of the torches glanced and flashed before my eyes, I clung to the arm of my Algernon, and looked to him for the interpretation of such singular phœnomena.

He made no reply, that I can remember, to my enquiries: but never shall I forget, the awful solemnity of his manner and appearance. With an endearing tenderness, he disengaged himself from my arms, and looked silently upon his sword, which he drew from his scabbard.

The mists and clouds in which I was involved, instantly vanished. I understood by this appeal, that we were pursued; that the heaven of heavens had withdrawn its protection from me, and that I was the author of a combination of evils under which my Algernon must unavoidably perish.

However, I assumed courage to witness the event, or rather took courage from the intrepidity and confidence which appeared to reign over the mind and imagination of Algernon.

Never did I behold him so patient and resigned, so cool and determinate. He appeared like one waiting the issue of an important epoch, but not of an expected calamity. He appeared a being of superior order, who leaves on the mind a stability and permanent character of security and courage, which is never acquired in the presence of the vulgar part of mankind. In short, he seemed to rise to sublimity; to soar above himself, or to ascend to a height far above all others.

But the courage of Algernon was not the only subject of my admiration. As the lights approached, he told me briefly, that he was convinced we were pursued, and in exhorting me to resolution, he employed a vigour of intellect, to which difficulties were temptations that awakened all his powers; that made him elevate himself to every exigence, yet without presumption or unworthiness, and that disposed him to meet the decrees of heaven, without amazement, terror, or confusion.

During the interval of these observations, the amiable L—d E———d was indefatigable: he placed the strength of his party at the pass; through which he presumed the pursuers intended to proceed, and he placed sentinels at such places as appeared capable of access, leaving me to the protection of Algernon, and in a spot the most likely to preserve us concealed.

These precautions were not of long avail. The unbroken solitude and lone situation we were in, was soon converted into a scene of uproar and blood.

I started; and directed Algernon's attention to a spot where we discerned the figure of a soldier move in the dark shade of the vast chasm, from whence the projecting brow of the rock on which we sat arose. The figure soon emerged from the darkened chasm on a part where the moon-beams shining between the trees, that waved in the breeze upon the surrounding crags, gave light to note the figure as it glided onward and vanished in the strong and gloomy masses of shade the cliffs above cast over the rugged declivities that wound between them. At every turn we eagerly followed it with our eyes; and when the rocks hid it from our sight, we remained in silent suspense till it emerged again.

I must confess to you, my Charlotte, although Algernon appeared composed, and insensible to every object but to me, whom he endeavoured to support, fortify, and encourage, yet did my mind fill with consternation and horror. And this spirit of credulity and superstition, was in no small degree augmentd by the many marvellous stories, strange and monstrous fancies, which I remembered to have heard told of the part of the country in which we were placed. I again believed all the imaginary tales, related for the amusement of my early youth, and I hung upon Algernon with a rooted persuasion, that the hill and the dale, and all around us were the nightly haunts of supernatural existents. With secret dread and uneasiness, I watched the re-appearance of the figure, or rather, with trembling horror I every instant expected its immediate approach. We heard steps: my perturbation increased. Algernon strove to embolden me.

"Be valiant-hearted, my Caroline," said he, "and above all, my lovely friend, suppress that superstitious awe which arises out of the melancholy solitude and extraordinary appearances that surround us. But, believe me, there is nothing more than human in these appearances, and as you perceive the lights are now all vanished, and the voices and figures no longer to be seen or heard, it is probable, that at the approach of day, we may be allowed to pursue our journey without interruption, and that the peace and blessings of heaven, may once again descend upon our heads. Observe, my love, how solitary! how silent!"

While thus speaking, our hearing was of a sudden invaded with the noise of numerous and unintelligible sounds. But silence again prevailed. We listened,—yet nothing, save the distant mur-

murings of the waters falling over the rocks, was to be heard. We looked anxiously around; still did not any-thing meet the sight, except dark and desolate rocks, that rose, as I before observed, in a vast sweep, cleft into many rugged chasms, from the spot where we stood. We examined the declivities, and found them so rugged and steep as to preclude all ascent or descent among them.

Alas! we were deceived. Our ears were again assailed by the voice of many persons in the apparent act of instantaneous approach. The figure, also, suddenly re-appeared. He rose from an unexplored avenue among the rocks, and elevating a torch above his head, its rays struck on the situation where we stood, and exposed us to his observation, and himself to our astonishment. He stood a moment in anxious deliberation, and then, with an agitated and hollow voice, called on me thrice by name——

"Caroline! Caroline!! Caroline!!!"

The deep and awful tone in loud echoes reverberated over the hills and dales, and, sinking in the distant air, all became silent, for an instant as before.

To my ears the voice sounded more than human, and I shrunk involuntarily on my knees, holding Algernon by the hand. But what was my terror and dismay, when other lights and other figures filled the scene; when cries and imprecations were heard; when the clashing of swords and the report of pistols rent the skies, and when Algernon rushed from my grasp, plunged into the bosom of the fight, and left me prostrate on the ground?

What was my terror and dismay? Ah, me! my Charlotte, vain question even to my own heart. Alas! I know not. I fell to the earth, and there remained till a solitary and painful silence again prevailed!

Recovering by degrees from this momentary death, this deprivation of mental sensibility, I heard my name again reverberating from rock to rock. Roused at this unlooked-for salutation, with eager gaze I turned my eyes in search of my Algernon, but saw him not!

I beheld, however, the figure before named, leaning upon his sword, and with his eyes anxiously bent upon me.

After a short and excruciating pause, he advanced with slow steps, and a high degree of perturbation and attention, to where I remained, chained by superstition and terror, on my knees to the rock.

Though in my breast imaginary fears were unusual visitors, yet the extraordinary occurrences, the uncommon situation, and the disappearance of my Algernon, of L—d E———d and of his party, oppressed my heart with sensations so strong that I relapsed into a state of mental derangement, and believed myself abandoned to the government of some tyrannic and supernatural power, determined to distract or to destioy me.

The figure now stood before me, with his countenance partially exposed to my view. I started at the sight of features I well remembered. The tomb in the grove, the remains of my grandfather, rushed upon my memory. I clasped my hands in agony. I called upon Heaven for protection. Fear and wonder possessed all my faculties, and I felt as if in the presence of a visitant from the grave. A chilling thrill stole through every vein, and reason yielded its throne to a terrified imagination and an affrighted fancy. But missing my Algernon, and gaining presumption from the desperation of despair, I shook off a portion of this infatuated weakness, and with an artificial energy, denoted by the tremulation of my voice, I addressed the phantom, as it stood silent and motionless direct before me.

'What art thou?' I exclaimed, 'comest thou of Heaven, or of the tomb of my grandfather, for thou dost bear the semblance of one the earth long since received into its bosom? Art thou his pure spirit? If thou art come from Heaven, I beseech thee, tell me where is my Algernon? Has he not been killed upon this hill? Dost thou come to tell me that he lives? Or, dost thou come to reproach me, as the cause of a father, or a brother slain? Oh, speak!'

I ceased. The figure waved his hand, and exclaimed—" Caroline! " Daughter! Unfortunate, abandoned, " disobedient girl, rise! rise, and follow " me! Cherish no further errors! Be " no longer ignorant. Your Algernon " and his banditti, while striking at " your father's, brother's, and friends' " lives, were destroyed or subdued. " Rise, girl! Follow your father, and " learn in future to love and to obey!"

I had conviction sufficient to discover that it was in truth my father. The fatigue he had endured, and the habit he was in, favored the delusion to which

I so long remained exposed. But it was in vain he told me to rise. "Algernon was destroyed, or subdued!" This dreadful fiat rooted me to the spot, and I must have been carried off the ground, with my senses bound in lethargy, or frantic with despair!

Adieu! Adieu!

CAROLINE.

LETTER XXXIX.

The rememberance I possess of what passed on my return to the Palace, is very imperfect.—I have a mere faint recollection of having stopped at the grove of the temple, and of contrasting the difference made in opinion by any change of the circumstances of our designs. How gay, how beautiful, how sweet was the delightful vale when I passed through it with my Algernon, but on my return, I thought, through the rustling air, a noon-tide pestilential vapour flew, and blasted all the fairy scene—spreading around a dire sepulchral gloom.

There is one circumstance, however,

which made too deep, too indelible an impression on my heart ever to escape my memory. I mean the manner in which I was received by my mother on my return to the Palace.

"Almighty God!" cried the venerable Duchess, sinking feebly on her knees, and raising her eyes and hands with meekly expressive devotion to Heaven, "Almighty Providence! "thou who never utterly forsakest "those who rely on thee, let the gra"titude of thy servant become accept"able in thy sight, both for restoring "my daughter to my arms, and for "giving her strength to resist the ca"lamities she has met and has to "meet!"

A deep heart-rending groan from me too soon convinced my beloved mother, that I was far, very far from possessing that strength with which she imagined my soul fortified.—Pale, agonized, faint, I strove to raise her from her knee. She rose, received me in her arms, and placed me on the sopha by her side; my head she received upon her bosom.

'Mother of my life!' said I; 'Mo-
'ther! ever intuitively the object
'of my tenderest affections!' continued I, with heart-broken sobs,—'tell
'me, dear Mother, have I lost for
'ever my Algernon? Does he live?—
'or is he dead? Speak! if dead, may I
'perish on thy breast; if living, let
'me bathe thy bosom with tears of
'happiness and joy?'

"He lives! he lives! my child," exclaimed the tenderest of mothers. I looked up to her eyes, I listened with eagerness to hear her further discourse, but she was silent, and her eyes, in spite of the constraint of her manner, filled with burning tears!

"He lives! he lives!"—I could utter nothing more my Charlotte, but I felt a reviving life flow rapidly to my heart, and almost overcome me with the excess of its impetuous volutions.

'He lives!' exclaimed I, 'Dear 'Mother! tell me where?—To tell 'me he lives is a great deal, I allow, 'yet, to a nature like mine, which 'would know all and every thing rela'tive to such a man, relative to my 'Algernon, it is not nearly sufficient; I 'would know where, how, under what 'circumstances he lives; and whether 'I may not once again—but once 'again behold him?'

"You are a frail being, my Caro-
" line," replied the dear woman, " you
" are compounded of extremes, and
" so abstracted that you live alone for
" your Algernon's love, involuntarily
" forgetting that you have a mother
" who has always entertained for you
" the most disinterested affection and
" maternal tenderness."

I pressed the hand of my mother to my lips. Conscience, duty, nature, and religion, united with my mother to make me sensible of the force of her gentle condemnation. I was about to speak, but could utter nothing coherent. I hung upon her and sobbed as if my heart would break. She kissed my forehead; pressed me to her breast, and told me she would relate to me the particulars of my capture and the circumstances attendant on my retreat.

" When we discovered in the morn- " ing," said my Mother, " that you " had absconded, that you were lost to " us, perhaps for ever, the cry of the " people was against your poor father's " cruelty, in driving you to so much " despair,—for alas! no circumstance, " just at first, came to light to lessen " the horror and misery we all felt in " supposing the desperate act you " took, was occasioned by your aver- " sion to the marriage with the Mar- " quis of Albion, and we were igno- " rant of the designs you might resolve " to execute.

" Your father suffered, I believe, " more than any other person. On " the morning of your flight he could " not endure to be seen: he thought " every finger made him its mark—every " voice whispered as he passed; and, " too surely, much of evil was at that

" moment imputed to him. Terrible
" it was to me, too, my child, to be
" compelled to conclude that I had
" lost my Caroline. Sweet sufferer!
" I knew you had been long lonely
" and unhappy but I could never sup-
" pose to such a degree as to urge you
" to despair or desperation. From
" what horrors of mind you would
" have saved both me and the Duke
" could we have been sure that you
" had not been impelled by despair
" to fly in the face of your God, and
" drag down our grey hairs with
" sorrow to the grave.

" Thanks be to Providence," continued my affectionate mother, " it was
" soon made certain to us, that you
" were seen on the road to the Mau-
" soleum in the grove, and although
" the return of Algernon was by no
" means understood, yet from the des-

" cription given me by our informant, " the person who made your disguise, " and who detected you in it, we " could have no doubt but that Al- " gernon and his friends formed the " party of your escort." 'Let us not " destroy the value of this discovery " by delay,' said your father: " saying " this, he directed your brother to ac- " company him instantly with a troop " of Light Horse, and, in a short time, " he departed bidding me not to des- " pair.

" Vain admonition ! He was not long " gone before I was looking every mi- " nute for his return. At length all of a " sudden the Palace yard was filled with " a concourse of people ; arms glistened " in the sun, and discontented mur- " murings, and dismal lamentations " appalled the ear ! Knowing the des- " peration of your passion, and quite

" fearful of every thing I should hear,
" I waited in agonizing suspence for
" the cause of the tumult in the
" court. At that instant your brother
" entered with his arm sustained in
" his scarf. I shrunk back !"

'Be not alarmed, dear Madam,' cried the sweet youth, 'there is no 'blood of any consequence spilt. 'Algernon favored by the loves and 'graces fought nobly. In the first in'stance the prospect was bright on 'his side—on ours all was gloomy. 'He gave me this wound and my foot 'slipping in blood I fell to the ground. 'My father, like a lion enraged, then 'attacked him. Algernon parried, 'but never thrust. I was rising 'from the earth to succour our party 'who were pushed to extremity by 'the people under the command of 'L—d E——d. My arrival encou-

'raged them: they defeated ther enemies, but L—d E——d cut his way through, and rushed to the assistance of Algernon, who was closely pressed by my father and two of his officers who came to his assistance L—d E——d, seeing that his friend merely parried with my father, was about to strike at the Duke's existence, when Algernon exclaimed——

"Fly! E——d, fly!—leave me to my destiny."

'On this he dropped on one knee, and presented my father with the hilt of his sword.—The gallant youth has received some scratches; he is now a prisoner in the Tower, and it is my father's decree that he shall remain there in irons till the hour that announces Caroline the wife of the Marquis of Albion. As to Caroline

' she was in an insensible state during ' the affray. My father has remained ' behind to succour and to guard her. ' They will of course travel slowly, ' but be not alarmed, you may expect ' their safe arrival every instant.

" Thus ended your Brother's nar- " rative," continued the Duchess, " you therefore see, my Caroline, that " you have not only to rejoice for the " preservation of his life, but have to " be thankful that Heaven has accord- " ed you the power of restoring him " to liberty !"

' Of restoring him to liberty!' exclaimed I, with an expression more of vague amazement than of direct significancy.

" Yes, Caroline !" said my Mother, " it is your first duty to restore him to

" liberty—cost what it will! Remem-
" ber, my child, that you professed to
" love him. Let that remembrance
" fortify your mind. Let it appeal to
" your heart. Let it demand—is it
" shewing love to the object of our
" affections, to suffer him to pine in
" gloom and solitude; to bleed in mi-
" sery and chains?"

Notwithstanding the cloud of melancholy which was visible on my distracted countenance, I could not suppress the dismal pleasure I derived from this convictive argument; and, without saying any thing in reply to my Mother, I could perceive that she encouraged a glad presentiment, that the generous love I entertained for Algernon, would never allow me to consent to a long continuance of his imprisonment. Under this impression she conducted me to my chamber, where I was confined for several days from excess of personal fatigue and mental lassitude.

During this interval the utmost activity was employed to precipitate my wedding with the Marquis of Albion, and when I appeared abroad my ears were assailed with congratulations, and my sight blasted with preparations for the pompous ceremony which was about to be performed.

This was but little fitted, my Charlotte, for the recovery of my peace of mind.—Instead of the joys of Hymen, such things only painted the guilt of broken vows, and the dreadful penalty that awaited them.—To me the songs of triumph which were perpetually to be heard, were discordant and terrifying sounds which appalled the ear, and made my blood chill within my veins.

Even from society I could not conceal my sensations, but often wept bitterly, and often smiled with the ghastly characteristics of a broken heart, or an hysteric affection.

My presence spread a gloom on the spirits of every company which neither wit, nor love, nor wine, could repel.— To avoid involving you in the like melancholy I conclude, &c.

CAROLINE.

LETTER XL.

It is the duty of a daughter to participate in painful recollections; and this plea will impose it on you to attend in particular to the important remainder of this correspondence.

You must recollect the state in which I described myself at the conclusion of my last letter: well, my Charlotte! I had not emerged from that state, nor had the report of my unfortunate flight been bribed or hushed into oblivion, before the Proxy for the Marquiss of Albion arrived, attended by a princely suite and two ladies of distinction.

The circumstances under which this fatal marriage was brought about, are not by any means sufficiently understood. I shall relate them in a few words:

On his marriage with me his debts were to be discharged: convenience then was the ground-work of his consent, and so ignorant was he of my principles and of my passion for another, that he expected I would give my hand to his PROXY with delight, and fly into his presence with almost maddening admiration.

Alas! he little knew; the world little knew, what contrasted emotions were the hopeless companions of my bosom.—But so convinced was he that I could not be inauspicious to any of his views, that he took no manner of pains to win me to his arms; so little, that one of the ladies sent by him to arrange my person was a favorite who had endeavoured to debauch his mind, and corrupt every amiable and virtuous feeling of his heart.

This profligate adulress is yet in existence. She is the author of all my degradation and despair! At the day of reckoning, and her account is large, she will find her persecuting spirit towards me, and towards you, my daughter, recorded against her in characters of living fire.—I shall nevertheless do her justice: believe me, the following sketch of her early life, does not proceed from a malignant, partial, or illiberal pen. Rely upon its truth and purity.

The name of this infamous Countess excites such a multitude of terrific ideas in my mind, that I fear I cannot pro- ceed with my usual precision and regu- larity.—Posterity will, I trust, do me justice by execrating her memory. And although posthumous justice cannot be heard by me, by the suffering indivi- dual, yet will it rectify the mistaken opinions which now prevail among my cotemporaries, and call down the bles- sings of a generous people upon my head, and the curses and execrations of an indignant multitude upon that of my depraved, perverted, and abandoned opponent.

Perhaps it will scarcely be believed, that at the commencement of the nine- teenth century, I should have been dri- ven from my Palace, and separated from my husband and his family, by the in- trigues of a noble prostitute, or that my life was rendered unsafe, and the legitimacy of my child disputed, through the mischievous suggestions of a public adultress, whose testimony is not held valid in the courts of honor, equity, or justice !—But I should not anticipate the events of my memoirs. I return to my subject.

This Countess is one of those singular women, who, before they attain woman-hood, lay by the innocent attributes of youth ; who lay behind them in their nurseries, the amiable tenderness, the unsuspecting openness and thoughtless generosity of unsuspecting age, and who came into public life with the depraved reason, the perverted religion, the cool caution, and prudent reserve which usually are bought by a long course of continued prostitution and obdurate profligacy.

This "LOVELY Countess," for so she is called, answered with the quickest improvements of the mind to the cares which were bestowed upon her education. The lustre of her beauty was also said to be indescribable. Unhappily, however, the partiality of her doting parent, a poor clergyman of Ireland, and the universal admiration paid to her person, intoxicated her young and thoughtless mind. She refused with unbecoming disdain, many honorable offers of marriage from private gentlemen, and, at a very young age, she conferred her hand upon Lord ———, a nobleman for whom she entertained both contempt and aversion!

How strange!—By no means. Lord ——— had wealth and titles and a disposition so tractable that it was understood and expected that he would never attempt to traverse the Countess's pleasures, pursuits, friendships, or designs.

Yet the "LOVELY Countess" had a susceptible heart, and had been much affected by the persevering assiduities of an illustrious admirer, who perpetually occupied her thoughts, and prevented every wish.

She loved splendor, and the richest jewels of J——s were found in the interior of her cabinet!

Flowers were her delight, and she saw, even in winter, the rose and jessamines of the east bloom among the rugged cliffs of her residence!

If she spoke of dress, her drawers were filled with the richest silks from

Persia, and with gold and silver muslins from the Indies.

If she thought of her generous lover; if she breathed a wish for his presence, instantly his manly figure blooming with youth and health, appeared before her, kneeling at her feet, or revelling upon her charms.

For some time every scene was a scene of unmingled happiness. The lovers were inseparable.—Participating in the power of the Marquis, the Countess extended her sentiments to all around her. Love and beauty followed her presence, and age and insensibility, in the form of a F———— were banished from the dwellings of "the BLESSED."

But a storm was arising to blast this fairy scene.—The creditors of the Marquis were clamorous for their demands. And his father would not consent to their discharge, without the Marquis consented to marry an illustrious foreigner of distinction, and remove from his arms those licentious and extravagant women who were the authors of his debts.

The Marquis consented to his father's terms.—The Countess flew to reproach him. She was received with a frigid politeness. Her countenance for the first time wore symptoms of displeasure. She remonstrated with the Marquis on his approaching inconstancy;—accused him of violated oaths, and was about to disappear with an indignant frown—when, recovering her serenity, and resuming all her native blandishments, she exclaimed——

" But no, Marquis, it cannot be " true that we separate. It cannot be " true that we are to cease to love, or " to be grateful to each other. I have " a remedy to prevent such an outrage. " You shall marry the Princess of Has- " burgh who is so much talked of; I " will proceed with your proxy to her " father's court, ingratiate myself into " her affections, mould her to my pur- " pose, be appointed the principal of " the ladies of her household, and by " this means secure an honorable and " legal title to live under the same roof " with you."

The Marquis was confounded and silent.—I know not what objections he made to this shameful proposition.

Indeed it is too much for me to know, that the Countess acted upon it, ignominious as it was; and that, from the day she arrived in my presence she commenced an attack upon my happiness, which menaces to afflict and degrade the remainder of my days.

You may well conceive, my dear maid, that I was not acquainted to the extent of these particulars on the instant of her first introduction to me: but I can assure you that my ignorance was shortly dissipated, and that the "lovely Countess" in a very few days appeared to me as the sepulchre of every virtue, and the mausoleum of every crime.

I am no uncandid antagonist, however;—in speaking of this lady I shall bend to the unclouded radiancy of truth, and am the first to admit, that had her early friends acted with my spirit and candour towards her, she could never have merited such animadversions as these.

They were much to blame. With the poison of flattery, they contaminated every good propensity of her soul: and destroyed that amiable diffidence which throws a soft and winning grace over all actions performed under its influence.

To the absence of this interesting quality is to be attributed much of the Countess's enormities through life. It has rendered her so intrepid, that she never becomes the victim of necessity, and it is believed, that since her persecution of me, she is so far from being embarrassed with humane sensations, that she would be more puzzled to account for their existence, than by any other difficulty proposed to her solution. Indeed, the fact is, she has much the same ideas of sentiment, that a blind woman has of colours, or a deaf one of sounds.

This callosity, this hardened impudence, pervades even her voice and conversation. And yet timidity in our sex, my Charlotte, particularly in speech and gesticulation, is, perhaps, one of the principal attractions which we are allowed to possess.

She who trembles in voice and limb when she begins to speak in a large society;—she who is overwhelmed with fear and diffidence when she converses on science and politics;—she who starts at the effect of her own eloquence, will be cheered and encouraged by the men, while the masculine address of the Countess's superiority of impudence, will call down indignation, and spend its fury without the triumph of admiration, or the advantages of success.

It is true, nevertheless, that with all this depravity and assurance, Lady ——— has passed with impunity through life, has not as yet—like a much more amiable woman the late D——— of D———e, been written down to the grave.

But I announce, that no insolent enemy of the House of Hasburgh, a house which I consider the particular glory of the German empire, and the peculiar pride of the human race, shall be suffered by me to invade its character and its rights with impunity.

The House exists no more! Alas! 'tis but too true. It is now a neglected exotic in a barren land; but it shall, nevertheless. be my duty to correct the outrages of licentious impudence, and to raise a monument to my house; such a monument as shall be consulted as a subject of sorrow, and as a source of truth! This idea oppresses me. For the present I conclude.

CAROLINE.

LETTER XLI.

No evil, my Charlotte, being so insupportable as that which is accompanied by consciousness of guilt, it soon became apparent from the procedure of "the Countess" at our court, that she possessed a mind gangrened with disappointment and remorse; shocked at the past, trembling at the present, and fearful to contemplate the future, it knew not on what to rest, or where to look for consolation and encouragement.

Overwhelmed with jealousy and chagrin, she eagerly listened to the first offers of relief. The infamous calumniators of the great assailed her!

She united herself to their confederacy. Like one that had no longer any confidence in herself, she was glad to repose her trust in any other that would undertake to guide her.

At this particular period, the mind of "the Countess" was wrought up to a pitch of fury, which scarcely could have been exceeded, had I been her most implacable enemy. She perceived that the numerous ambassadors and foreigners of distinction, who visited my father in consequence of this intended alliance, treated her with the most sovereign indignation and contempt; while they paid their homage to me with an extraordinary degree of admiration and respect, and seemed disposed to report me to the Marquis of Albion as a Princess, endowed with more elegance of mind, suavity of manners, and dignified graces, than they had hitherto met with in the German states.

These praises were certainly more general than merited. However, such as they were, the Continent echoed with them, and made me, during the agitation of the union, the perpetual subject of adulation and applause.

This generous conduct of the public towards me, excited the most wanton rage in the heart of "the Countess." And the direction which she gave this rage, was the most mischievous that could be devised by malignant ingenuity. To give full effect to this diabolical passion, and finding my life and morals irreproachable, she determined that calumny should be diffused by all the most industrious arts and methods of propagation; that nothing should be too gross, or too refined, too cruel, or too trifling to be practised:

that no regard should be had to the rules of honorable hostility; that every weapon should be accounted lawful; and that if she could not destroy my reputation, she should injure me by a petty malevolence, or wound me with feeble blows and repeated, though impotent charges. That is, if she could not assassinate by force, to poison my cup, and give me a protracted and wretched existence!

Not that she meant to use such vulgar instruments as the dagger and the bowl. No, my Charlotte, the Countess has the merit of having improved the means of inflicting human injuries, and of making use of a power more subtle and more pliable than the poison, or the sword. She attacks with a weapon more cold and deadly; with an instrument that pierces the heart without the mark of blood; that palls the hand which aims the blow, and covers the designs of the flagitious enemy.

It must be confessed, then, that her proceedings on so important a mission amply justify the character I have drawn of her in my last letter. But I find, my dear girl, that emotions of my mind, cause my pen to wander. I should have told you, that "the Countess" commenced proceedings, by cultivating a particular intimacy with me, in order to draw from my breast those secrets which she thought necessary for he establishment of my future infamy and misery.

In compliance with so atrocious a determination, she courted my society without having any desire for my friendship And without being humble, she followed my footsteps, tended my table, assisted my toilette, attached my sandals, and appeared to delight in contributing to my pleasures and enjoyments. No method did she leave untried to rifle my secrets. My autbority she treated with abject submission; my pride, she soothed with the most plebeian humility, and my habits and sentiments, she applauded with the most profligate adulation.

But there is no part of my intercourse with this dangerous woman that has made so deep an impression on my mind, as a particular conversation which I held with her one morning on the subject of my illustrious alliance.— Having wormed me into confidence by the radiancy of her flattery, and the brightness of her manners, I candidly told her that, though I might be compelled to marry the Marquis of Albion, I could never be disposed to love him.

'No, never!' exclaimed I, 'and I 'am therefore convinced that an union 'formed under such a circumstance, 'must be attended with more linger- 'ing pains of heart, more anguish of 'mind, more tears of repentance, and 'more agonies of despair, than can 'possibly be imagined or conceived.' I had no sooner concluded this sentence, than the Countess smiled with ineffable grace, and said——

"You must be under some delusion "or mistake, amiable Princess! the "object of a political marriage is not "love or affection. Your only object, "then, will be, to revel in the splen- "dour of your husband, who, in his "turn, will enjoy the honors of your "alliance, leaving himself, as well as "you, to the free indulgence of such "sentiments as you may both have

" formed, in the more early and sym-
" pathetic periods of your lives.

" You are by no means to under-
" stand," continued the Countess, with all that witchery of expression which she can assume when she thinks proper to fascinate or to charm,

" You are not to understand, lovely
" Princess, that this political marriage
" will draw an insuperable line of
" separation between you and the
" objects of your love or esteem. In
" an union of such a nature it would
" be absurd to talk of affections, or to
" conceive, that either of the contract-
" ing parties is to be held in the capti-
" vity of those who unite their hearts,
" their fortunes and their beings, after
" a long and personal acquaintance,
" and an intimate knowledge of each

" other's peculiar virtues, and distinctive charms.

" Besides, in no country is jealousy carried to such little excess as in England. The nobility, in particular, of that country have too much liberality to oppress each other with the bondage of chains. Their beautiful females, after marriage, enjoy the most unbounded freedom; go where they think proper, and visit, or are visited by, whom they please. They are under no manner of constraint or reserve, and are allowed to possess the supreme controul over their sentiments and affections."

'What! after marriage!' interrupted I, with an expression of horror and astonishment.

" Yes!" continued she, " yes!—
" after marriage!—The English nobi-
" lity, of the highest order, have con-
" ceptions so extensive and philosophi-
" cal, that they never suffer the viva-
" city of their affections, or the fire of
" the heart, to be stifled by the obli-
" gations of matrimonial contracts—
" which were only intended to bind,
" and cement together, the ignorant
" and vulgar portion of mankind.

" Therefore, my charming Princess,"
continued the Countess, " when you
" marry the Marquis, and feel disposed
" to tenderness, the voice of nature,
" of a kind and beneficent nature, is all
" that you will have to attend or to
" pursue; and whatever awakens your
" sensations, gratifies your desires, il-
" luminates the imagination, and con-
" tributes to your enjoyments, you will
" be left at full liberty to attain. You

"may amuse yourself with what society "you think right, without imagining "that you are to suffer that ardour to "consume you which now animates "your youthful mind."

Her eyes were fixed upon me, and she perceived the blood mantle upon my cheek. But she was mistaken The emotion was not what she supposed. I thus undeceived her——

'Infamous resources!' exclaimed I, 'miserable indemnifications for a blot-'-ted reputation and broken vows;—'sooner would I suffer my soul to con-'sume in its own fire, than to temper 'its violence by illicit applications or 'illegal indulgences!'

The Countess appeared anxious to interrupt me. I allowed her to proceed.

"The error is," replied she, "in "your not comprehending the differ- "ence between a marriage of policy "and of the heart. In a marriage of "the heart, the observance of fidelity "is a virtue; in a marriage of policy, "the breach of that fidelity is consi- "dered no crime. The nobility of "England are so well aware of this, "that their jealousy is never offended. "They know that confidence cannot "be reposed in the discretion of per- "sons who unite, more for conveni- "ence and interest, than for senti- "ment. Faithful to nature, they wink "at infidelities which they know to be "the merited recompence of mercenary "engagements; and, as I before ob- "served, enchanting Princess, when "you marry, you will feel yourself at "full liberty to follow the trend of "your most ardent inclination and "desires."

In this manner did the Countess endeavour to exaggerate the incontinence of the English nobility, no doubt with the view of debauching my mind, and of veiling over the enormities of her own heart.

Tired of the negative felicity she herself experienced from matrimony, she broke the most solemn obligations, and abandoned an amiable husband, and the beauties of virtue, to glut the cravings of a perverted appetite in the arms of such as could stoop to the gratification of the vicious and depraved sensations of her blood.

And fearing that if the Marquis were to marry a woman of a character likely to attach him to fidelity and domestic endearments, the opportunity of satiating with him her hungry intellect, would no longer be accorded, she desired that I should hold the holy rights of matrimony in derision and contempt, without conceiving such conduct as the source of sorrow, or as the most prolific subject for remorse.

'And is adultery among the English 'nobility, Lady ——,' said I, 'un-'limited, and unattended with the pu-'nishment and shame which is attach-'ed to that guilt by all the other civi-'lized inhabitants of the earth?'

"I have given you my reasons," answered the Countess, "for extending "indulgence to political and distin-"guished alliances."

'It is in vain, my Lady,' interrupted I, for I was shocked and fatigued with her perverted morality, 'it is in vain 'for you to exhaust any further on the 'subject, I look upon adultery as the

'crime the most shameful to the per-
'petrator, and the most dangerous to
'society. For I consider the marriage
'contract as the grand basis of civil fe-
'licity; as the fundamental principle
'of public happiness, and, at the same
'time, of individual comfort and pros-
'perity.'

She made no reply to this, but before I conclude this subject, I will make one remark directly to you, my dear and amiable Charlotte.

Believe me, believe a mother who has your dearest interests at heart, that whoever shall design to impair, pervert, or bring into contempt the marriage contract, strikes at the moral constitution of a government, and deserves to be prosecuted and punished with the utmost zeal of religion and rigour of the law.

To cut down the banks and let in the sea, or to poison all the springs and rivers in a kingdom, cannot be considered near so mischievous as undermining the foundations of matrimony; for physical evils only affect the present age, whereas those of a moral nature extend to the remotest times, and ruin and enslave posterity.

For my own part, there is no crime I contemplate with more horror than the crime of adultery, nor any title I hold in such abhorrence as that of an adultress.

I can pity the gaunt and ragged prostitutes who prowl about the streets for the purpose of supporting a miserable existence; I can suffer to see those creatures who haunt our theatres and public walks and gardens, and I can pass over the conduct of the wretched whose miseries plead some excuse for the infamy of their lives, but I cannot extend either humanity or indulgence to the ADULTRESS; to the malignant ADULTRESS, whose crime involves her own family in disgrace and desolation, and that of the ADULTERER in consternation and horror!

But I am truly weary of the reflections I have been led into by this abandoned woman. I wish to speak to you further of Algernon—Perhaps in my next I may have that indulgence.

CAROLINE.

LETTER XLII.

I HAVE had no direct occasion, my dear girl, to make mention of Melina for a considerable time, but I can now assure you, that she was seldom absent from my presence, and that during the remainder of my stay in Germany, I had every reason to thank Heaven for having indulged me with so interesting a companion and so faithful a friend.

Melina was not allowed, no more was any other person who had not my father's cypher, to visit Algernon, but Prince L—s, whom the Duke could not refuse with propriety, obtained the cypher every day, and reported to me or to Melina the conversations which he held with our dear and mutual friend; for Melina continued to love him with the tenderest affection; and, although she was convinced of the impossibility of a reciprocal passion, still did she continue to reject the advances of Prince L—s, and resolve to die in possession of those genuine affections which were the pride and animation of both our breasts.

Never was there a more interesting woman than Melina, and her passion for Algernon was so pure, that it corrected the former levity of her character, and shed such a brightness over her life, that it was impossible to know —and not to love and to admire her.— As you may well conceive, her conversations with me had but one subject, one prominent feature—my passion for Algernon.—In our first intercourse after my unfortunate flight, Melina delighted in affording me encouragement.

"By fortitude and valour," said she to me on the day of my return, "men subdue their enemies; and by "patience and perseverance they over-"come the stupendous works of na-"ture, which has elevated mountains in "vain to stop the progress of him who "is determined to conquer."

But no sooner did the noble proxy, and "THE COUNTESS," with the rest of the suite arrive, then Meliha ceased to dilate my heart with hope; on the contrary she began to prepare my mind for an union with the Marquis.

Unhappy Union! Like an unseasonable blight, it came upon me and levelled all my happiness to the dust!

—But to marry the Marquis, was to redeem the captivity of Algernon!—Could I hesitate to strike off his chains when the power was thus placed in my hands?—Being disappointed in blendiny my fate with Algernon's, my cup of misery was filled to the brim, my marriage. therefore, with the Marquis could only affect the quality of the ingredients—not the quantity of the dose, and it would enable me to acquire an antidote for the poison in the liberation of the man I loved.

Amid the ruin of my felicity there was but one tie left to hold me to the world,—the freedom and the happiness of Algernon, was the tie which was to cheer and maintain my future existtence!

For his sake, then, for the sake of Algernon, did I consent to marry the

Marquis, to struggle to live, and to support with a resignation becoming a Princess and a Christian, the sorrows that rived my heart, and shook my mind to its very centre.

But, notwithstanding, the prudent and disinterested nature of these resolutions, I was determined once more to behold Algernon; to bring him tidings of my sentiments; to mitigate his destiny, and to prove to him that I was not to obtain HIS freedom without assuming to MYSELF the chains of degredation and captivity.

To contrive this awful and interesting interview, I directed Melina to consult with Prince L——s, and to devise a plan remote from frustration, disappointment, or discovery.

Melina communicated my intentions to the young Prince, and he as instantly came into my presence.—Nothing could equal his distress and astonishment on finding me determined to persevere in the resolution I had formed of visiting the Tower. He commenced his visit by endeavouring to turn me from so dangerous and impracticable a purpose, but perceiving that all he could say would be totally fruitless, he attended to what I had to observe to him in speechless despair.

'Oh! bring me to Algernon,' said I, 'my dear Prince, conduct me to the 'prison of Algernon!—Let me survey for the last time the first object 'of my affections! Let me pass the 'barriers which now separate me from 'him, and I shall look with averted 'eyes at the mountains which the tyranny of a father—determined to ele-

'vate between us.—Dear Prince! be 'not so obdurate, let me behold Algernon, before these eyes are closed 'in endless night;—before—idea still 'more horrible!—before——I could not proceed.

The air of sensibility and determination with which I uttered this, softened the soul of the Prince: and after a short struggle between a sense of duty and the cries of Nature, he abruptly said:

"Be it so, Madam, my part at this "moment shall not be that of an officer "who considers nothing but his duty "—it shall be that of a man who considers nothing so obligatory as "soothing the unfortunate and exercising kindly offices for a friend. You "shall see Algernon. I will confide "to you the cypher of the Duke.

"Prepare a disguise; and as the si-
"lence of the night is favorable to your
"contemplation, I recommend you to
"prefer it to the glare and tumult of the
"day. Take Melina as your compa-
"nion. I will follow at a distance: be
"confident of my devotion to your
"safety and obedience to your com-
"mands. Let the hour be one of the
"ensuing morning. Farewell!"

Thus did this amiable Prince yield to my entreaties, and cause my heart once more to beat with a doubtful delight, and my eyes to sparkle with a factitious pleasure. Doubtful and factitious!—See the event!

The sensibility of your tender nature, my Charlotte, is more than sufficient to inform you, that I trembled in silence for the moment that should conduct me to the prison of Algernon.

—Never did I pass hours of such excruciating solicitude. To relieve the agony and tedium of so painful an interval, I proposed a walk to Melina, and we were no sooner abroad than our steps involuntarily led to the Tower which contained that object which was held by us so sacred and dear.

The Tower stood on the brow of a rock overgrown with briers and thistles, and was inaccessible except at one side, where there was a steep ascent of one hundred steps to a stupendous portico with iron folding gates, guarded by centinels of the regiment of guards.

On the summit of the portico stood a figure of white marble, which I could not look upon without horror. And yet it was the figure of Justice; but so affrighted was my imagination that I beheld only the sword and the rod, and saw nothing of the milder attributes, the scales and the balance, which it poised in its opposite hand.

I shall be too prolix, my dear girl, if I attempt to describe any further object or emotion of this agonizing interval, I shall therefore hastily conclude this letter, and in my next detail the important interview. Till then, &c. &c.

CAROLINE.

LETTER XLIII.

At length the anxious, the much looked for hour arrived, and I once again left the splendour of a palace to visit the gloomy abode of my beloved Algernon. I must pass over the mechanical arrangement of this enterprize, my admission into the Tower, and the attendant circumstances, and contending emotions naturally connected with so intricate and daring a design.

I say, my Charlotte, I must pass over all preliminary detail, and rapidly inform you, that after being conducted through a variety of winding passages, and up a tremendous flight of steps to the top of the Tower, Melina and I came to a door which stood open, and before we beheld Algernon, I heard his voice murmuring in feeble complaint. I heard him sigh as though his heart would burst.

We ventured to advance a little. He started, and the chains rustled upon his limbs. Their terrific tinkling shook the palsied element of the apartment, and every thing trembled in unison with the heart-rending sounds.

By the light of a lamp, which cast a feeble beam upon his countenance, I perceived him sitting with his head reclined upon his arm. I approached with inexpressible emotion, a few steps nearer to him. He rose, alarmed, but without seeing me, and walked slowly towards the door; his feet encumbered with irons, and his left arm wrapped up in his scarf.—I sank into the chair which he had abandoned, and Melina, equally overwhelmed, dropped on her knees and sobbed aloud.

This was a language which could not be misinterpreted, or unheard in the situation in which we were placed. It not only penetrated the ears, but the heart of Algernon, for he instantly turned his head, and uttered an exclamation, which fully denoted his conviction of my presence, and the extreme agitation of his mind.

"My Caroline!" he exclaimed, precipitating his shackled steps towards me, and sinking into my arms,——

"You are here! Heaven be praised!
"my fears were groundless. Indeed!
"Indeed! I trembled lest some vio-
"lence—lest some treachery, or tyran-
"ny, should have compelled you to

" abandon the unfortunate Algernon to
" all the horrors of captivity and de-
" spair."

The delusion under which I perceived he existed, penetrated my heart with the most poignant sorrow, and bewildered my reason so much, that in the destruction of the delusion, I employed as little preconcerted caution as apparent sensibility. I abruptly replied——

'Alas! Algernon, your fears were 'not groundless! My hand is promised 'to the Marquis, and I have consented 'to become his wife, on condition 'that————'

Without waiting to hear the conclusion of this sentence, Algernon burst away from my embrace, and as he traversed the chamber with feeble and lingering steps, I could perceive an entire change operating upon his manner and mind. The few words which I uttered, suddenly blunted the edge of sorrow, and the hardy nature of the soldier, assumed dominion over the winning softness and amiable graces of the man. Endeavouring, however, to recover more evenness of disposition, and to suppress the sudden starts and throws which convulsed his bosom, he again turned towards me, and said— with a tone awful as firm——

" Did you not pause, Madam, did
" you not take a moment for reflection,
" before you promised your hand to
" the Marquis? Did you not balance
" one instant on my destiny; or did
" you immolate me with a remorseless
" cruelty and guilty indifference? When
" you agreed to marry the Marquis;
" when you pronounced upon me a

" sentence worse than the stroke of " death, was your heart as cold as " your words were perjured?"

He paused, and bending his eyes directly upon me, seemed to wait a reply. But I was silent: filled with stupor and amazement, I gazed upon him with a wild insensibility, and, without any attempt at interruption, suffered him to continue to outrage my feelings, and harrow up my soul.

" What are your motives, Madam," continued he, " what are your views, " what are your prospects, for what " end do you marry the Marquis of Albion? What are your induce- " ments? Is it love, think you? No! " Love is a noble and generous passion, " and can only be founded on a pure ' and ardent friendship, on an exalted " respect, on an implicit confidence

" in its object. Search your heart, " examine your judgment: do you find " the semblance of any of these sen- " timents to bend you to the Marquis? " What, then, can degrade a mind, to " which nature and education has " given such port, statue, and charac- " ter, into a concurrence, or consent " with such an union! Can you re- " pose any confidence in yourself? are " not you at this instant come to take " a farewel of a lover, to whom you " are solemnly allied? Horrible union! " If it take place, both you and the " Marquis will be as dead to the sense " of conjugal as of parental obligation, " and you will abandon each other's inte- " rests and offspring with as little scru- " ple as you abandon me at this present " hour. Look then well to the step " you are about to take, for, however " you may behold it now, be assured it " will lead to a conduct which you

" will hereafter acknowledge to be
" blackened by every aggravation!"

'Hold! Sir, hold!' interrupted I, in frantic agony!

'Hold! Sir, is it no circumstance of
'mitigation, is it no palliation of guilt,
'that I have consented to marry the
'Marquis on the direct condition, and
'for the particular purpose, of restor-
'ing you to freedom and to your coun-
'try? I sacrifice myself for you! I have
'consented to a miserable captivity, in
'order to set you free!

'You tell me to weigh well my con-
'duct! Alas! I know well the risque
'I am running in a stranger, when I
'meet with reproach from you! My
'anxiety for your happiness, has made
'me overlook every consideration, and
'induces me to commit my destiny to

'a man whom I have never beheld, 'and who probably will unite with you 'in reprobating me, for a measure in 'which I see nothing but the most vir-'tuous and disinterested sacrifice. A 'sacrifice, which I thought would 'claim from you the most kind and 'exalted sentiment of tenderness, and 'in which the most fastidious rigour 'must find so much more subject for 'sympathy, than for blame.'

He rose his hand from the table, advanced a step or two, and was about to reply to me.

'Stop, Sir,' continued I, 'let me 'first ask you, can you answer for such 'cruelty towards me; or, was our in-'timacy so joyless, so loveless and un-'endeared, that you have lost the 'sense of its happiness, and forget of 'what dispositions I am formed? But 'you never knew, or you cease to 'know me! Let me ask you, did I 'not, with all the resolution of strong 'faith, fling my youth, my rank, and 'my hope upon your bosom? Did I 'not weigh you against the world, and 'find it light in the scale? Did I not 'take you as an equivalent to the 'wealth and titles of that world? And 'do I not now abandon that bright 'equivalent, in order to make you free? 'Let me ask, have you proven your-'self worthy the sacred trust I reposed 'in you? Has your spirit so associated 'with mine, so as to leave me no 'room to regret the splendid and dis-'interested sacrifice I had made? And 'does my soul find a pillow in the 'tenderness of yours, and a support in 'its firmness? Do you preserve me 'high in my own consciousness, proud 'in your admiration and friendship, 'and happy in your affection and 'esteem?'

He approached insensibly to me, dropped upon his knees, and seized my hand.

'But why should I proceed?' continued I, still smarting under the sense of his reproaches, 'perhaps it was original pride, and a wish for greatness, 'by which you were actuated, and 'that love for me was an artificial acquirement, which varnished before 'the original impressions of nature. 'Your unfeeling charges against me, 'bear witness to the truth of this horrible suspicion. You forget too, what 'you found me, and———.'

Here he could no longer restrain his emotion, and as he rose his head from my lap, where he had rested it, I discovered that he had been absorbed in tears.

" No! Madam," exclaimed he, in accents of the deepest despair, " no!
" I do not forget how I found you, nor
" am I insensible to the state in which
" you are placed by me. I found you
" a fair and blushing flower, its beauty
" and its fragrance bathed in the dews
" of Heaven. But I no sooner beheld
" it, than I interrupted its nutriment,
" and, without cutting it down, or
" placing it in my bosom, I have left
" it to be rifled by one who may waste
" its sweetness, blast its beauty, and
" bow down its faded and sickly head!
" And how do you punish me? I, who
" am the author of your principal calamities, how am I punished? Alas!
" by the noblest condescension and
" endearing kindness; by a visit to a
" prison, and by restoring me to liber-

" ty—to enjoyment! But how have I
" requited you, angelic Caroline? By
" scoffing taunts and degrading suspi-
" cions! Yet odious and contemptible
" as so barbarous a conduct must make
" me appear to you, I am not altoge-
" ther so odious and contemptible as
" you imagine. I was ignorant, O
" Caroline! I was ignorant, that in ac-
" cepting the hand of the Marquis,
" you were swayed by the intention of
" breaking these chains and of casting
" me free. Pardon me, then; sup-
" press your indignation and abhor-
" rence, and be disposed to feel for the
" deplorable condition to which I am
" actually reduced, and the still more
" deplorable one which I have pros-
" pect before me, if my restoration to
" freedom must be purchased at the
" expence of your liberty."

'O rise, Algernon! rise!' said I, 'for
'I do forgive you; from my heart for-
'give you. Let us no longer remain
'in this painful error, or waste a mo-
'ment, stolen for your consolation, in
'misunderstandings and displeasure.'

He rose, but again sunk upon his knees, and pressed my hand to his lips, more with the convulsive emotion of despair and agony, than with that of love.

I prevailed on him to rise, I rose myself from my seat, but not having strength to maintain myself, I fell, nearly lifeless into his feeble arms.

Melina could not remain a silent spectator of this painful scene. She advanced to console and to uphold us. But she lost her resolution in our sorrow; in the place of mitigating, she heightened and confirmed all our grief.

" What a progress, dear and adorable " friends!" said she, " have you to " travel through, before you can obtain " the peace and tranquillity which you " have lost! How like the wounds of " the body are those of your minds! " How burning the fever! How pain- " ful the suppuration! How slow, how " hesitating, how relapsing the process " of convalescence! Through what va- " riety of sufferings, 'through what new " scenes and changes must you pass,' " before you re-attain that health of " heart, of which you have been de- " spoiled by the cold and political pro- " position of a gilded stranger! How " could the Duke become so hardened " as to attend to this proposition? To " abandon you both in the bloom of " life to different destinations, and to "see those hopes for ever blasted, "which you once cherished! How can "he expose you to so unmerited a fate? "How can he commit such a crime as "to separate such faithful, such tender "and affectionate lovers?"

Sobbing with agony, and weeping on each other's breast, we mutually turned our eyes upon Melina, but they were shortly after attracted to another object.

Prince L—s, impatient at our long stay, and dreading the fatal consequences, determined to interrupt the interview, and with that resolve suddenly entered the apartment.

He had no occasion to announce his remorseless design. We too well divined it, for Algernon pressed me closer to his heart, and I involuntarily exclaimed, 'O we must part! Farewell! A long farewell!

Prince L—s would afford no opportunity of further explanation. Algernon appeared about to speak.

" Reply not," said the prince, " Al-
" gernon, be a man!"

With this, he tore me from the breast of the tenderest of all lovers, and bore me out of the room.

I was just sensible that Algernon fell upon his knees, and addressed himself—not to me, but to Heaven! I can trace back nothing further of this interview, my Charlotte, I can only remember the horror with which I was struck in treading back the mazes of the tower, thro' which I passed on my way out, and the tangled wilderness which appeared to obstruct my return to my apartments in the palace. Every thing appeared contrived to mislead and to perplex me, to affright and to astonish. I at length found myself secure within my chamber, but it was in vain that I endeavoured to seek for repose. No sooner did sleep approach me, than scenes of wanton cruelty rose up before me, and I passed the remainder of the night, and following morning in a manner never to be described. Farewell! my Charlotte.

CAROLINE.

LETTER XLIV.

On the morning after the mysterious and heart-rending interview, I was directed by my father to attend him to his closet.

The voice is the organ of the soul: I soon discovered that the Duke laboured under some secret cause of dissatisfaction: had he been more affectionately disposed, I might have taken courage to expostulate against the union with the Marquis, but his expression, manner, and appearance, concurred to convince me that the attempt would be fruitless, and that any obstructions on my part, would not only be vain and ridiculous, but instrumental to the further hardship and imprisonment of Algernon. For my father no sooner placed me by him, than he commenced, in the following imperious and broken style, to communicate with me.

"I shall not, Caroline, perplex my "thoughts, or waste my time, in saying more to you than that I have "ordered your union, by proxy, with "the Marquis of Albion, to take place "to-morrow morning, and as I have "reason to expect some treachery has "been lately, and may again be employed, I shall detain vengeance "in my hands; that is, I shall hold Algernon in chains, with the sword of "justice suspended by a thread over "his head, till I hear of your arrival in "England, and of your conducting "yourself with respect and complacen-

" cy towsrds the illustrious house to " which you are about to be allied.

" Make me no reply," continued the Duke, thinking that I was about to oppose his will, " make me no reply girl. " I am acquainted with your daring " conduct of last night. I have sent " Prince L—s to Berlin, Melina is con- " fined during pleasure. You are now " destitute of accomplices, and venge- " ance is in my hands! You can con- " cert no further schemes, nor cherish " any further extravagant hopes. Obey, " therefore, and obey chearfully, and " I shall not only restore Algernon to " my favor after your reception in Eng- " land, but I shall promote him to the " highest dignities, and take upon me " the advancement of his fortunes."

Here the Duke ceased.

I own to you, my dear Charlotte, that this amiable intention respecting the suffering Algernon, revived all my grief, and I felt more sensibly affected than when I heard him spoken of in the dreadful language of threatening vengeance. This spoke some comfort to me, but I could not repress my tears, nor avoid seizing my father's hand and imploring him to watch over the future happiness of his unfortunate prisoner.

The Duke took me to his arms, tenderly kissed me, and told me, that I had only to obey him chearfully, and that I might rely upon his restoring Algernon, not only to freedom, but to his former friendship and favor.

I interceded at the same time for Prince L—s and Melina, and with success. After which the Duke gave me permission to retire, not, however, without repeating the overwhelming assertion, that it was essential I should hold it well in my remembrance, that vengeance was to remain in his hands, till after my alliance with the Marquis and the return of a courier from England.

Thus left without a choice, or rather thus inhumanly restricted, I resolved to make a merit of necessity; to assume a chearfulness sufficient to veil over the gloom of my heart, and to confer freedom on Algernon with as little reluctance and delay, as might be consistent with the ruin of my own happiness and the loss of my own liberty.

Passing to my own chamber from my father's study, I was accosted by my mother. There appeared in her eyes and countenance so deep an expression of sorrow, arising no doubt from a knowledge of my conduct the preceding night, that my mind immediately filled with the most agonizing penitence, and had she not supported me in her arms, I must have had sunk to the earth, and contributed still more to that affliction with which she was already but too sensibly overwhelmed.

From the sobs and broken sentences which escaped me, as I hung around the neck of my mother, she had no difficulty in comprehending what had passed between me and the Duke, and she appeared delighted to find, that my desire to accelerate the freedom of Algernon, would enable me to support the ceremony of the proxymial wedding, and to pass through the remaining ordeal with becoming complacency and resolution of mind.

She also conceived this to be a favorable opportunity of impressing my mind with a sense of the important duties of a wife, who wished to preserve the esteem of her husband and of society: with this intention she conducted me to her library, where we found Melina and the Countess of ———, and she admonished me in the following manner: I give her own dear words directly as they flowed.

"The most likely way, my Caroline, either to obtain a good husband, or to keep one good, is to be yourself good, amiable, and just.

"Avoid, both before and after marriage, all thoughts of managing your husband. Never endeavour to deceive, or to impose upon his understanding, nor give him uneasiness, as some do very foolishly, to try his temper; but treat him always before-hand with sincerity, and afterwards with affection and respect.

"Be not over-sanguine before your marriage, nor promise yourself felicity without alloy; for that is impossible to be attained, not only in your particular state, but in the present state of things. Consider, before-hand, that the person you are going to spend your days with, is a man, and not an angel: and, if when you come together, you discover any-thing in his humour and behaviour, that is not altogether so agreeable as you expect, pass it over as a human frailty; smooth your brow, compose your temper, and try to improve your condition by a gentle and chearful good-nature.

"Remember always, that whatever misfortunes may happen to either, they are not to be charged to the account of matrimony, but to the accidents and infirmities of human life; a burden which each engages to assist the other in supporting, and to which both parties are equally exposed. Therefore, instead of murmurs, reflections, and disagreement, whereby the weight is rendered abundantly more grievous, readily put your shoulder to the yoke, and make it lightsome to both.

"Resolve, every morning, to be chearful and good-natured that day; and if any accident should happen to break that resolution, suffer it not to put you out of temper with every-thing besides, and especially with your husband.

"Dispute not with him, be the occasion what it will; but much rather deny yourself the trivial satisfaction of having your own will, or gaining the better of an argument, than risque a quarrel, or create a heart-burning, which it is impossible to know the end of.

"Be assured, a woman's power, as well as happiness, has no other foundation than her husband's esteem and love; which, consequently, it is her undoubted interest, by all means possible, to preserve and increase. Do you, therefore, study his temper, and command your own; enjoy his satisfactions with him, share and sooth his cares, and, above all, my Caroline; and, above all, with the utmost diligence, conceal his infirmities.

"Read frequently, with due attention, the matrimonial service, and take care, in doing so, not to overlook any of its solemn obligations.

" Always wear your wedding-ring; for therein lies more virtue than is usually imagined: if you are ruffled unawares, assaulted with improper thoughts, or tempted in any kind against your duty; cast your eyes upon that ring, and call to mind who gave it you, where it was received, and what passed at that solemn time.

" Let the tenderness of your conjugal love, be expressed with such decency, delicacy, and prudence, that it may appear plainly and thoroughly distinct from the designing fondness of a harlot.

" Have you any concern for your own ease, or for your husband's esteem? Then have a due regard to his income and circumstances, in all your expences and desires; for if enormous debts should follow, you run the greater hazard of being deprived of both.

"Let not many days pass together without a serious examination how you have behaved as a wife; and if, upon reflection, you find yourself guilty of any foibles, or omissions, the best atonement is, to be exactly careful of your future conduct, and to determine to sin no more."

In this manner did my amiable mother conclude her rules and maxims, for the promotion of matrimonial happiness. During the interesting recital, she was attended both by me and Melina, with the most dutiful attention, and by "the Countess" with the most unblushing impatience and unveiled disapprobation of every aphorism she heard uttered. Captious and petulant, she instantly rose as my mother concluded, saying, as the time had been considered wasted in Germany, she hoped the ceremony would be performed early on the morrow, and that I would make it convenient to depart without further delay.

This dreadful annunciation revived all my sorrows: I even feel its influence at this distant period, and am too much affected just now, to say more to my Charlotte—than adieu! adieu!

CAROLINE.

LETTER XLV.

I SHALL not consume your attention, my Charlotte, by going into a description of the ceremony, by proxy, which united me to the Marquis, and which, at the same time, separated me from every object that was dear to me upon the earth.

In truth, were I ever so much disposed, I am not qualified to convey any correct idea of the performance, and the whole tenor of my conduct during the ceremony, must have contradicted any hope that my acquiescence was not extorted instead of being voluntary.

Incapable, however, as I am of describing the mechanical arrangement of the ceremony, I feel too lively a sense of my feelings on that occasion not to be competent in some measure to express this poignancy.

Never can I forget the moment when I was conducted to my father into the hall appointed for the scene of my misery. Every eye was upon me; and while a splendid and awful concourse with fixed attention, and filled with I know not with what expectancy, gathered round me to watch my every expression and catch my every word, I laboured, not with guilt, but with perplexity, and was so little capable of replying to the congratulations of the numerous audience with common propriety, that it exceeded my capacity to speak at all, and I hurried from one object to another with the precipitation of folly, or rather with the silent perturbation of a criminal accused of the most heinous crime.

But when I came to accept the hand of the proxy, and to violate those vows which I made in the presence of Heaven to the unfortunate Algernon, I felt as if I was charged with the highest sins; with an enormity for which I wished to suffer death;—a crime, to the commission of which there appeared to me to go far more insensibility of heart, more profligacy of morals, than I thought ever could have fallen to my lot.

This was not an impression to be long endured: it soon caused a faintness to come over me, and I was compelled to leave the hall the instant the ceremony was fulfilled.

For a little space I was confined to my bed, and when I rose, I was so macerated and enfeebled, that I could make no resistance to the plan which had been formed for hurrying my departure to E——d, there to confirm the vows I had but just made.

To aggravate my calamity, I was not suffered to bid farewell to Algernon.

No eager pleading on my part could win my father to consent to accord me this indulgence.

Denied this last consolation, and all matters being in readiness, I commenced my journey for E——d, attended by my brother, Prince L——s, Melina, and my household servants, and followed by the two ladies, the gentlemen and the numerous train of the Marquis of Albion's splendid establishment.

I know of nothing interesting that occurred on our route to embarkation: indeed the tender rememberance of the friends I was about to abandon, the lamentations which I heard reiterated along the road for my departure, and the improbability of my ever again beholding my beloved mother, my father, my friends, or my country, all contributed to sink me into the deepest gloom and despondency; and, if I betrayed attention to any object, or addressed myself to any person, those circumstances were accompanied with sudden starts and a harshness of manners and expression, which bore evidence of a temper soured by disappointment, or of a heart overflowing with rancour or grief.

In this state of mind I arrived at the place of embarkation where the last act of agony was to be performed.

I mean the taking an eternal farewell of my country; of my brother; Prince L——s; Melina, and a few other attached friends who followed me to the sea-shore.

This was a severe trial; a trial that required the utmost fortitude to endure.

To abandon the Palace of my ancestors, the land of my birth, the authors of my life, the friends of my bosom, and the man of my heart; to abandon all those dear and sacred connections, and to embark on a new and tremendous element for the purpose of precipitating myself into the arms of a strange man, a strange country, and a strange people, was, I believe, such a trial as was never before suffered by any other mortal; nor is it, from the change effecting in the political state of things, by any means probable, that it will ever be endured by any other person again.

I predict myself to be the last victim of that infamous policy which makes matrimony a mercenary and political, not a moral and religious engagement.—But this is not the place for this discussion, I therefore hasten to observe, that Melina was the last dear object of my embrace, previously to my embarkation. To her I confided all my little remembrances, together with a ring, which I took from my finger, and which I conjured her to deliver to our dear and mutual friend, the unfortunate Algernon. Her reply was sunk in sobs and tears. With streaming eyes we bid an eternal adieu;—she and her friends to return to the palace, and I, surrounded by strangers, to proceed on board ship, and cast myself upon the mercy of total strangers—perhaps prejudiced foes!

This was not a step to be taken without lingering and sorrow. The spot on which I separated from Melina possessed so much attraction, that to leave it appeared to me more painful than the pangs of death. It was situate on a high cliff on the very edge of the sea. On one side a large tract of land extended itself, finely diversified by stately trees, floating corn, and pasturage for cattle. On the other side rolled the great and wide sea, which I had never beheld before, where go the ships, and where is that leviathan, whom the Almighty Creator has made to take his pastime therein.

Which way soever I looked, I met with subjects for astonishment; I saw new footsteps of the divine immensity.

I viewed the novel and marvellous works of an Omnipotent God, whose labours I had before only witnessed, confined to the narrow circle of my native country. Every thing, therefore, which I encountered, gave me ten thousand additional arguments to fear his tremendous power, and at the same time to love his diffusive goodness.

I thought of my friends and of my home, and I anticipated the horror of going amidst strangers, and the dangers attending the deep abyss, but again I thought, how safe are they who have so infinite and mighty a Being for their guard!—How happy are they who have so inexhaustibly rich a God for their portion! But how wretched, how miserably, and emphatically wretched, are those who have such a God for their enemy and avenger!—Oh! can our feeble frame, exclaimed I, that shrinks at a little light affliction that is but for a moment,—how can it bear the never-ending vengeance of that prodigious arm, which stretches out the Heavens, lays the foundations of the earth, and pours out the waters of this mighty deep which now expands before me?

If such were my reflections while comtemplating the ocean from a rocky eminence, you may well conceive the alarm and agitation I was in when I found myself, for the first time, sailing upon its heaving yet magnificent surface. And yet, I can assure you, as soon as I lost sight of my friends, and recovered in some sort from the agony into which I was cast, on no longer beholding even the land of my nativity, I became apparently reconciled to the novelty of my situation, and able to form some opinions upon the persons and circumstances surrounding me.

The exercise of sailing, struck me at the time, as being from its passive nature, extremely favorable to feeble and valetudinary subjects. From the efforts I made to keep myself from falling, I found every muscle brought into exercise, by which means the blood was preserved from stagnation, and the perspiration increased and carried off by the constant change of atmosphere in the ship in perpetnal motion.

The air too appeared to me to possess uncommon virtues and properties, which consisted, perhaps, in its being freed from those noxious animal and vegetable effluvia, which abound in the air of inland and confined countries.

Novel and interesting, however, as every scene and circumstance was to me, they made no manner of impression upon the mind of any other beholder. And to my utter astonishment, the ladies flirted with the officers with as much vivacity and ease as if they were in the antichamber of a court, instead of treading the quarter deck of a king's ship subject to the action and dangers of the ocean.

Indeed the Countess seemed to exult and to enjoy her situation.—But when she discovered that C——n P——e, who commanded the frigate, directed all his attention to me, and that every gentleman in the ship was anxious to mitigate my sufferings, by every little office of respect and kindness, her spirits began to droop, and her manners became tainted with the characters which are thought to denote a jealous or malicious soul.—I shall pursue this voyage in my next. Till then farewell!

CAROLINE.

LETTER XLVI.

THE wonders of my first voyage, my dear Charlotte, were not a little excited by the multitude of ships which I saw sailing in every direction, and carrying on the great mercantile business between E——d and all other civilized countries. As my ideas on this general kind of commerce were very imperfect, I applied to C——n P——e for information, and he replied to me in the following satisfactory manner:

" In a philosophical point of view, " Madam," said he, " much has been " said for and against this great com- " merce of G—t B——n. Narrow- " minded moralists expatiate largely

" against the evils with which it fills " society. They dwell with a pleasure " that shall not hastily be called mali- " cious, upon the thought, that, at " some former period, tea, coffee, and " chocolate were never tasted, except " in great and rich families: but, now, " the articles of tea and sugar are in " common use; we send to the East " and West Indies to furnish our poor " with breakfast. The wives of day- " labourers, and the very alms-house- " women drink tea twice a day!—But " I remember a more rational com- " plaint was made by an Indian of Lou- " isiniana, when he said that, in his " country, the young men overworked " themselves to procure baubles for " their wives, which Europeans had " introduced.—That luxury, the off- " spring of commerce, is a colossal " monster, who, from his cradle up- " ward, spreads social disorder and in-

" dividual wretchedness, is, however, " a fact not less true than serious; " and, did any-thing the word exhi- " bits, authorise us to believe that " human life was intended to keep that " unagitated course, which it is one dis- " position of the mind to desire, we " might load it with unqualified exe- " cration: but, since man appears to " be innately active, and, in all situa- " tions, exposed to evil, we may sur- " vey with a less heated imagination, " activity of this particular kind, and " evil of this particular form. To " commerce, with all its mischiefs, " with all its crimes, committed upon " every shore, its depopulation of " fields, and its corruption of cities,— " to commerce we must attribute that " growing intimacy between the mem- " bers of the human race from which " great benefits have redounded, and " greater still may spring.—Commerce,

" on the whole, Madam, is highly fa-
" vorable to the intellectual part of
" man, and perhaps, as injurious to the
" animal: it multiplies his ideas and
" his wants; brings riches to nations,
" and poverty to individuals, making
" the rich poor, and the poor, ' poor
" indeed.' In nations under these
" circumstances, it has been justly ob-
" served, every man that does not turn
" his talents to account, will find him-
" self left behind in theu niversal emu-
" lation."

C——n P——e had just come to the conclusion when his attention was called off by some object relating to his duty. As I shall have frequent occasion to mention this gentleman in the remaining part of this correspondence, I cannot just now employ myself better than in conveying to you some faint idea of his character.—Neither the parents, nor the education, nor the fortune of this eminent seaman, would have conferred on him any distinction in society, or in his profession, had not nature conferred on him a portion of genius that soon distinguished him from the vulgar herd.

Seemingly doomed, by inevitable circumstances, to the regions of the cock-pit, or, at most the ward-room, he yet found means to emerge from that situation; to obtain the rank of c——n, then a——l, and, when on shore, to move in the highest circle of distinguished life. This rise was considerably accelerated by the protection of the Marquis of Albion; for the Marquis was his early friend; was the first who admired his talents, pointed his efforts and taught him to aspire at fame and fortune. Indeed such was his conduct towards him, that with a friendship bordering on enthusiasm, he transformed the seaman into a courtier, appointed him master of his horse, and honored him with the commands of trust and confidence.

But this unexampled goodness had no manner of evil influence over the mind or manners of C——n P——e. When at court he was nothing more than a gentleman: when at sea he was nothing more than what ought to be the commander of a ship of war. In this duty he was indefatigable, and, in time of danger, was ever seen in places the most dangerous. His accommodations, with the exception of the arrangements made for me, differed but little from the common crew, no one, therefore dared complain, and all was harmony and affection under his command.—In regard to his discipline, whether an enterprize was possible or not, when he ordered an undertaking, every one did his utmost to execute it, full of confidence in him. He knew how to take away any thoughts of doubt from the minds of his seamen. His orders had nothing conditional in them.—'run under that fort; board that ship; cut out that vessel'—These were the terms in which his directions were given, and yet at the instant of entering his cabin after the most violent and apparently tyrannical conduct on his quarter-deck, his manners became suddenly complacent, and his conversation affable and affectionate as could possibly be.—To me he was particularly kind and respectful; anticipating all my wants, and endeavouring to relieve the ENNUI of the voyage by the introduction of anecdote and such amusements as a ship of war could afford.—But finding me on the second night of my voyage particularly low-spirited; afflicted with a sick head-ach and but little disposed to retire to rest, he proposed to me to walk on the quarter-deck, and amuse myself with the contemplation of the stars. I complied.

At no time, my Charlotte, could I behold the dread magnificence of Heaven without emotion, but the instant I beheld it reflected from the bosom of the deep, and understood from C——n P——e, that it was the only true guide of navigation, I could not view it without feeling the most earnest solicitude to learn every thing respecting it that the powers of the mind could discover.

So absorbed was I in admiration of the scene, that my imagination became romantic, and I could not resist addressing the C——n in the following eccentric manner:

'I see the stars rising from the East 'in endless succession; and I feel 'that nature, who has linked the 'lot of man with so many invisible 'objects, has surely given him a rela-'tionship to those that present them-'selves to his eyes. And do you think, 'Sir,' continued I, 'that we are not 'connected with a scene, from which 'we receive not only the sublimest, 'but the clearest conceptions of the 'creation, and its Creator?—Nor do 'you find that its vastness oppresses 'us: let us now watch the impression 'it makes upon, and observe whether 'it does not rather prompt us to claim 'a kindred with the skies?'

Perceiving that I took so much delight in the contemplation of the heavenly bodies, C——n P——e recommended me to accompany him on the poop, where, with the assistance of a night-glass, I could enjoy the scene to infinitely more advantage. Having reached the poop, and seated myself on the signal chest, I again addressed myself to C——n P——e, who stood close to me with the glass in his hand, through which he pointed out to me by name the different planets, and I said to him————

'What a melancholy thought it 'would be did we look at those stars, 'and believe that they should continue 'to revolve through an eternity after 'ourselves were lost in nothingness!— 'but this is not the spontaneous, and 'therefore not the instinctive feeling 'of Man. On the contrary, how natu- 'ral, how congenial to the heart, at 'least how congenial to my heart, to

‘ exclaim—When thou sun of Heaven shall fail; if thou shalt fail; ‘ thou mighty light; if thy brightness ‘ be but for a season, like that of the ‘ unfortunate Caroline’s, still my name ‘ shall survive thy beams.’

It required no uncommon degree of penetration to discover from this exclamation that my mind was disposed to revert to former objects and to sink into a deeper melancholy.

To avert this consequence and to restore my imagination to a proper bias, C——n P——e took up the conversation, and, laying his hand upon my arm, said———

“ It is true, amiable Princess, he “ that has made himself acquainted “ with the heavenly bodies, is enabled “ to behold with the mind’s eye, a

" prospect, in which this our globe
" forms but a small part indeed! and
" it is impossible to think justly, on
" those three great objects of all
" thoughts,—Man, the world, and the
" Diety, without beginning at this
" point. The low theology of the an-
" cients arose out of astronomical ig-
" norance. To their eyes the earth
" was a plane; beneath its surface was
" the abodes of the dead; above it,
" rose the vaulted skies, at once a ca-
" nopy to men, and a habitation to the
" gods. The shining stars ornamented
" the Heavens, as the flowers did the
" fields, and the world was not a part,
" but the whole.

" But what are our conceptions,"
continued my interesting instructor;
" reclined as we are on the stern of
" this vessel, and looking at once into
" the ocean of universal space?—We

" suppose this space unbounded ; be-
" cause with the idea of boundaries
" we must connect that of something
" beyond those boundaries, and this
" can be nothing but a recommence-
" ment of space.—We therefore con-
" sider ourselves resting upon a body
" that is perpetually turning round, and
" to which we adhere by the unaltera-
" ble nature of matter. We reflect
" that if a bird, or a balloon *could* rise
" to the height at which the attractive
" influence of the earth ceases, it must
" fall into the void.—We reflect that,
" could we divest ourselves of matter,
" we should be released from that
" power by which we are chained to
" the earth : and having supposed this
" alteration, we may please ourselves
" with the thought of our liberty, or
" trembling, that, as the world turns
" round, we shall drop from it into the
" dark and chill space that we conceive

"unbounded. But there is no such
"space, Beyond our horizon there
"commences, indeed, a space of the
"nature of which we can give no ac-
"count, further than that it is the
"space in which those stars are placed.
"And those stars, as you have observ-
"ed, are the centres of systems; that
"is, points, round which their attending
"planets revolve;—suns, by whose
"power those planets are enlightened
"and warmed:—and are not these
"stars, in their turn, but parts of still
"larger systems? Is there not a point
"round which they, with all their
"worlds in harmonious order, revolve,
"and which is, to them, a sun, similar
"to that which illuminates our earth?"

I was about to reply to these interesting observations, but was interrupted by some person coming upon the POOP and calling upon me by name. It was

" THE COUNTESSS" and just as she advanced to the stern she discovered me, together with C——n P——e, who was employed in wrapping a boat-cloak round me to preserve me from the inclemency of the night air.—On beholding us she uttered an exclamation of astonishment, and retired, hastily begging pardon for having interrupted our conversation or repose.

Without discovering the extent of her meaning, what she said was sufficient to remind me that the night was far advanced, and I retired to my cabin, but without the smallest comprehension, that I had that night committed an error, which would taint and embitter the fame and happiness of my future days.—How could such an imagination come into my head? Could I have passed the hours more innocently? And was not the companion of those hours the Marquis's most faithful and particular friend. Could any calumny be more wild and extravagant than that which should attempt to attach guilt to me and to a man under such circumstances? Notwithstanding every improbability, it will appear to you hereafter, that calumny did make this night an instrument for my destruction:—but of this hereafter, my Charlotte, of this hereafter.

CAROLINE.

END OF VOL. II.

M. Allen, Printer, Paternoster-Row, London.

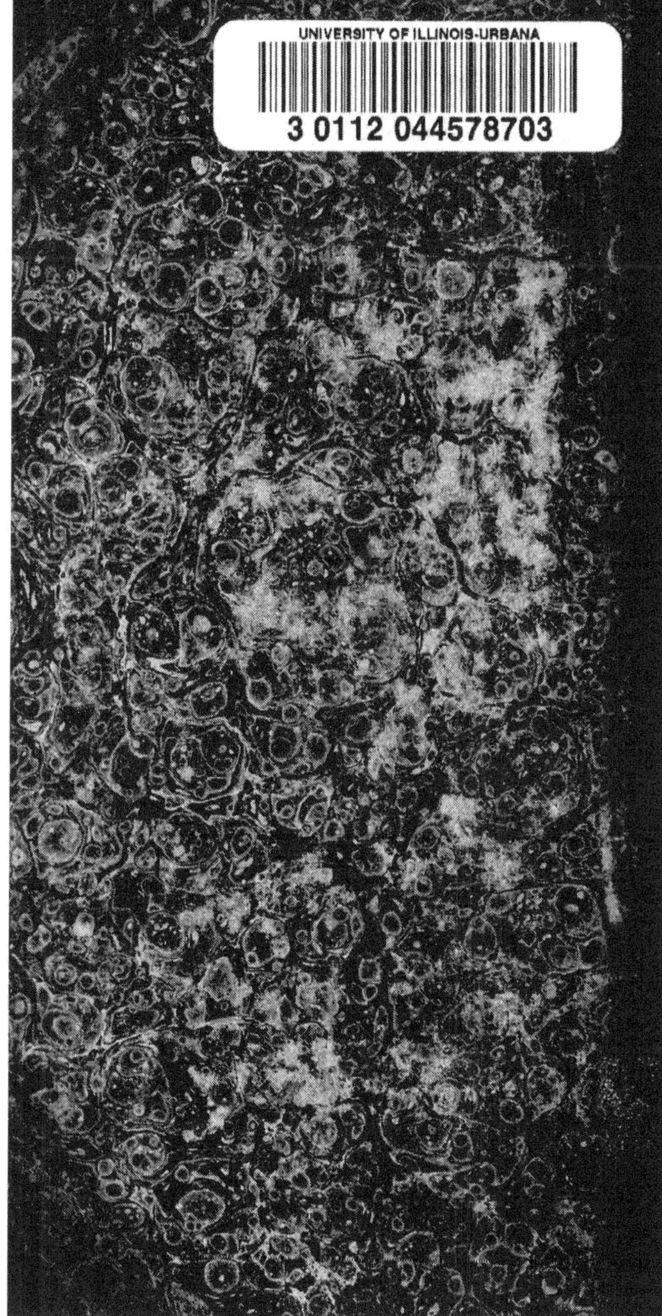

CPSIA information can be obtained
at www.ICGtesting.com
Printed in the USA
LVHW041421200123
737508LV00008B/527

9 781371 116774